CONTENTS

	Page No.
Editorial	2
Notes	3
Section I PHQ Cards (GB)	4
Section II Guernsey Cards	20
Section III Jersey Cards	20
Section IV Isle of Man Cards	21
Section V Benham 'Silk' Cards	22
... Postal Region	37
South Eastern Postal Region	44
South Western Postal Region	52
Wales & Marches Postal Region	57
Scottish Postal Region	61
Northern Ireland Postal Region	64
National Postal Museum	65

N.B. Many Post Office Cards — particularly the PHQ series of cards, are available with special commemorative postmarks. Full details of all these postmarks are given in "COLLECT FIRST DAY COVERS" published by B.B.P. Publications Ltd., and available from most Booksellers, Stamp Dealers or Royal Mail Philatelic Counters (at principal Post Offices) price £3.50.

© Benham (A. Buckingham) Ltd. 1987

No part of this publication may be reproduced by any means whatsoever without written permission from the publishers.
SBN. NO. 0 947901 05-1

Possibly the first G.B. Commemorative Postcard. This one costs £30.00.

EDITORIAL
COLLECT POST OFFICE CARDS 1987
ALSO INCLUDES PO COMMEMORATIVE COVERS AND BENHAM 'SILK' CARDS

A notable date for collectors of Post Office cards was 1 October 1986 when a major restructuring of the Post Office created three separate businesses – Letters, Parcels and Counters. The abolition of the nine regional headquarters in Great Britain on that date marked the end of 'Regional' cards as we have come to call those picture postcards issued by the Regional Boards. This 6th edition of our catalogue, which includes all known issues of regional cards spanning a period of twenty years up to the very last one issued on 30 September, may now be regarded as the definitive work on this subject. As indicated in the last edition, this year's listings contain additional detail incorporating more of the Regus catalogue information.

We shall await with interest the announcements of cards this year as it is understood that there are four main District offices for the Letters business and the same number for Counters, in addition to which the Boards for Wales, Scotland and Northern Ireland continue in operation. Whether these changes will result in picture postcards being issued by the Post Office nationally or by the District offices is unknown when this catalogue went to press. Catalogue listings will need to reflect the new organisation and it is predicted that there will be wider collector interest in Regional cards as the completion of a collection by basic catalogue numbers is now achievable. It was also announced that the new managing director of the Letters business would have responsibility for philately but that Counters would have control of the philatelic counters. Whatever the changes we see in the marketing of cards, commemorative covers and stamps 1987 will be an interesting year for collectors of all items sold over Post Office counters.

The popularity of both the National Postal Museum and PHQ 'stamp' cards appears to be growing but it must be stressed that in the case of unused cards one should endeavour to collect only those in perfect mint condition.

If there is aditional information on Post Office cards which you consider is worthy of inclusion in future editions of this catalogue we should be pleased to hear from you. All comments, even criticisms, are welcome in order that we may continue to publish a catalogue which you the collector will find invaluable for day to day reference.

A. ROBERTS

ACKNOWLEDGEMENTS

The assistance of all sections of the Post Office is acknowledged with thanks. Much additional information has been provided by both collectors and dealers over the years and we are very grateful for all their contributions.

NOTES CONCERNING USE OF THIS CATALOGUE

PHQ CARDS

The first section of this catalogue lists PHQ cards, the term "PHQ" stands for Postal Headquarters. PHQ cards are Post Office issued commemorative postcards that show enlarged reproductions of British Commemorative stamps from 1973 to date. The initial print figures for these cards wee a mere few thousand; issued occasionally as a cautious experiment, now, over a decade later, the Post Office produces these full colour cards for every issue in very considerable quantities.

The first two issues, 1973 Cricket and 1973 Inigo Jones, were 120/121 mm x 171/172 mm in size with all subsequent issues being approximately 104 mm x 148 mm.

The original Post Office selling prices for these cards were:
```
     PHQ  1-12    5p each      PHQ 39-48         8½p each
     PHQ 13-32    7p each      PHQ 49-56         11p each
     PHQ 33-38    8p each      PHQ 57-78         13p each
                               PHQ 79 onwards    14p each
```

First Day of Issue prices refer to the first day of the stamp shown and not the actual card as the card has no specific issue date but is usually on sale approximately two weeks before the stamp issue.

The print figures quoted relate to the total number of sets issued, e.g. for the London Landmarks set (PHQ43) 300,000 of each card were released.

The Special Handstamp price is a minimum price for a card in this category in good condition. Scarcer handstamps do command a premium over these prices.

POSTMARKS

Observe postmarks (i.e. on the front) command a premium in excess of postmarks on REVERSE (back of card) — with the earlier PHQ cards.

For a complete listing of the special postmarks normally available, we would refer you to the First Day Cover catalogue "Collect First Day Covers".

ERRORS

Errors (or misprints) on PHQ cards are rare as they are security printed and occur very infrequently. PHQ cards with missing colours are the most sought after and can be very effective. Approximate prices for such errors are as follows:
  Missing colours: £25-£100 (depending on effectiveness)
  Shift of colour: £2.50-£30 (depending on effectiveness)
  Printed on wrong side: £5-£15 (depending on issue)
  (Glazed reverse, matt on front)
  Reverse side blank: £10-20 (depending on issue)

SECTION 1 — PHQ CARDS

PHQ is the complicated key which simply means issued by Postal Headquarters. (P for Postal, H for Head and Q for Quarters – *very sophisicated).* This year we have decided to completely rethink the cataloguing of these attractive, beautiful Post Office Cards. We have always, in the past, tried to combine Mint with Used but this makes I think a very complicated catalogue system and also it is difficult to make generalisations when you are dealing with two completely different collecting habits. In future, we will devide into two, the first section will be for Mint Cards and the second for Used Cards giving far more information and help. We hope to expand this enormously during the next few years-

A) MINT PHQ CARDS

It is posible with Mint PHQ Cards to have very high standards. Perfect cards fetch a considerable premium but on dog-eared and bent ones such cards have little value. However, collectors can sometimes take things to extremes. At one time a dealer who specialised in cards used to have I think ten grades – they have long since gone bankrupt and to be honest I am not surprised. Anyone trying to sort out ten different types of Mint Card really deserved to go bankrupt. In general, there are only three types of cards – perfect Mint; those that have a slight fault and by this I mean a small corner fault, perhaps a slight surface scratch but nothing that will detract from the card and thirdly those that are completely unacceptable and, in general, I would not recommend anyone to collect these. The numbers printed of early cards are remarkably low, hence the high price. They were also destroyed at the end of the year as with the policy of stamps. This changed in the mid 70's which is another reason why the early cards are so very very expensive.

Prices of Mint Cards have remained remarkably stable right through the depression. There has been an enormous increase in interest in PHQ Cards and I feel that Mint Cards will not remain as low as they are for much longer. It would seem that 1987 will be a good year to fill up those gaps in your collection.

J. & K. KIFF

**REGIONAL, POSTBUS AND PHQ CARDS
ALSO NATIONAL POSTAL MUSEUM SS SERIES
AND BENHAM SILK CARDS
MINT AND F.D.I**

Send 1st Class stamp for a copy of our price list
**Kenwood House, Cottered, Nr. Buntingford, Herts. SG9 9PS
Telephone: 076 381 273   Mail order only**

			Price Perfect	Price Slight Fault		
1973, JULY	PHQ1 CENTENARY OF COUNTY CRICKET (1)		40.00	30.00	☐	☐
1973, 15 AUGUST	PHQ2 INIGO JONES (1)		65.00	55.00	☐	☐
1973, 12 SEPTEMBER	PHQ3 PARLIAMENTARY CONFERENCE (1)		25.00	20.00	☐	☐
1973, 14 NOVEMBER	PHQ4 ROYAL WEDDING (1)		12.00	8.00	☐	☐
1974, 27 FEBRUARY	PHQ5 BRITISH TREES (1)		80.00	70.00	☐	☐
1974, 24 APRIL	PHQ6 FIRE SERVICE ANNIVERSARY (1)		80.00	65.00	☐	☐
1974, 10 JULY	PHQ7 MEDIEVAL WARRIORS (4)		20.00	15.00	☐	☐
1974, 9 OCTOBER	PHQ8 SIR WINSTON CHURCHILL (1)		5.00	4.00	☐	☐
1975, 19 FEBRUARY	PHQ9 TURNER BICENTENARY (1)		15.00	12.00	☐	☐
1975, 23 APRIL	PHQ10 EUROPEAN ARCHITECTURAL YEAR (3)		5.00	4.00	☐	☐
1975, 11 JUNE	PHQ11 SAILING (1)		4.00	3.00	☐	☐
1975, 13 AUGUST	PHQ12 RAILWAYS, 150th ANNIVERSARY (4)		45.00	40.00	☐	☐
1975, 22 OCTOBER	PHQ13 JANE AUSTEN – BICENTENARY (4)		15.00	12.00	☐	☐
1976, 28 APRIL	PHQ14 SOCIAL REFORMERS (1)		4.50	3.50	☐	☐
1976, 2 JUNE	PHQ15 BICENTENARY OF AMERICAN INDEPENDENCE (1)		3.00	2.50	☐	☐
1976, 30 JUNE	PHQ16 ROSE SOCIETY CENTENARY (4)		20.00	17.50	☐	☐
1976, 4 AUGUST	PHQ17 BRITISH CULTURAL TRADITIONS (4)		7.50	6.00	☐	☐
1976, 29 SEPTEMBER	PHQ18 500th ANNIVERSARY OF BRITISH PRINTING (4)		7.50	6.00	☐	☐
1976, 24 NOVEMBER	PHQ19 CHRISTMAS (4)		2.50	2.00	☐	☐
1977, 12 JANUARY	PHQ20 RACQUET SPORT (4)		5.00	4.00	☐	☐
1977, 2 MARCH	PHQ21 ROYAL INSTITUTE OF CHEMISTRY CENTENARY (4)		4.00	3.00	☐	☐
1977, 11 MAY	PHQ22 SILVER JUBILEE (5)		12.50	10.00	☐	☐

N.B. As from PHQ23 all cards described as mint refer to perfect. Slight seconds 50% discount on most sets, or minimum 50p per set (otherwise 'sets' like PHQ76 at 20p would be 10p less than cost).

1977, 8 JUNE	PHQ23 HEADS OF GOVERNMENT (1)	2.50	☐
PHQ24 NOT ISSUED			
1977 5 OCTOBER	PHQ25 BRITISH WILDLIFE (5)	2.50	☐
1977 23 OCTOBER	PHQ26 CHRISTMAS (6)	2.50	☐
1978, 25 JANUARY	PHQ27 ENERGY RESOURCES (4)	2.50	☐
1978, 1 MARCH	PHQ28 BRITISH ARCHITECTURE (HISTORIC BUILDINGS) (4)	2.00	☐
1978, 31 MAY	PHQ29 ANNIVERSARY OF THE CORONATION (4)	1.50	☐
1978, 5 JULY	PHQ30 SHIRE HORSE SOCIETY CENTENARY (4)	2.00	☐
1978, 2 AUGUST	PHQ31 CYCLING CENTENARIES (4)	1.50	☐
1978, 22 NOVEMBER	PHQ32 CHRISTMAS (4)	1.50	☐
1979, 7 FEBRUARY	PHQ33 BRITISH DOGS (4)	2.50	☐
1979, 21 MARCH	PHQ34 BRITISH FLOWERS (4)	1.00	☐
1979, 9 MAY	PHQ35 EUROPEAN ELECTIONS (4)	1.00	☐
1979, 6 JUNE	PHQ36 HORSE RACING PAINTINGS (4)	1.00	☐
1979, 11 JULY	PHQ37 INTERNATIONAL YEAR OF THE CHILD (4)	1.00	☐
1979, 26 SEPTEMBER	PHQ39 150th ANNIVERSARY OF THE METROPOLITAN POLICE (4)	1.00	☐
1979, 21 NOVEMBER	PHQ40 CHRISTMAS (5)	1.25	☐
1980, 16 JANUARY	PHQ41 WILD BIRD PROTECTION ACT CENTENARY (4)	1.00	☐
1980, 12 MARCH	PHQ42 LIVERPOOL AND MANCHESTER RAILWAY 150th ANNIVERSARY (5)	1.25	☐

Date	Issue	Price Perfect	Price Slight Fault
1980, 9 APRIL	PHQ43 LONDON 1980 (1)	0.25	☐
1980, 7 MAY	PHQ43 LONDON LANDMARKS (5)	1.25	☐
1980, 9 JULY	PHQ44 FAMOUS AUTHORESSES (5)	1.05	☐
1980, 4 AUGUST	PHQ45 QUEEN MOTHER'S 80th BIRTHDAY (1)	0.50	☐
1980, 10 SEPTEMBER	PHQ46 BRITISH CONDUCTORS (4)	1.00	☐
1980, 10 OCTOBER	PHQ47 SPORTS CENTENARIES (4)	1.00	☐
1980, 19 NOVEMBER	PHQ48 CHRISTMAS (5)	1.25	☐
1981, 6 FEBRUARY	PHQ49 FOLKLORE (4)	1.00	☐
1981, 25 MARCH	PHQ50 INTERNATIONAL YEAR OF THE DISABLED (4)	1.00	☐
1981, 13 MAY	PHQ51 BUTTERFLIES (4)	1.25	☐
1981, 24 JUNE	PHQ52 NATIONAL TRUSTS (5)	1.25	☐
1981, 22 JULY	PHQ53 ROYAL WEDDING (2)	0.50	☐
1981, 12 AUGUST	PHQ54 THE DUKE OF EDINBURGH'S AWARD (4)	1.00	☐
1981, 23 SEPTEMBER	PHQ55 FISHING (4)	1.00	☐
1981 18 NOVEMBER	PHQ56 CHRISTMAS (5)	1.25	☐
1982, 10 FEBRUARY	PHQ57 CHARLES DARWIN (4)	1.00	☐
1982, 24 MARCH	PHQ58 YOUTH ORGANISATIONS (4)	1.00	☐
1982, 28 APRIL	PHQ59 BRITISH THEATRE (4)	1.00	☐
1982, 16 JUNE	PHQ60 MARITIME HERITAGE (5)	1.50	☐
1982, 23 JULY	PHQ61 BRITISH TEXTILES (4)	1.00	☐
1982, 8 SEPTEMBER	PHQ62 (2)	0.50	☐
1982, 13 OCTOBER	PHQ63 BRITISH MOTOR CARS (4)	1.25	☐
1982, 17 NOVEMBER	PHQ64 CHRISTMAS (5)	1.25	☐
1983, 26 JANUARY	PHQ65 FISH (4)	1.00	☐
1983, 9 MARCH	PHQ66 COMMONWEALTH DAY (4)	1.00	☐
1983, 25 MAY	PHQ67 ENGINEERING (3)	1.00	☐
1983, 6 JULY	PHQ68 BRITISH ARMY (5)	1.50	☐
1983, 24 AUGUST	PHQ69 GARDENS (4)	1.00	☐
1983, 5th OCTOBER	PHQ70 FAIRS (4)	1.00	☐
1983, 16 NOVEMBER	PHQ71 CHRISTMAS (5)	1.25	☐
1984, 17 JANUARY	PHQ72 HERALDRY (4)	1.50	☐
1984, 6 MARCH	PHQ73 CATTLE (5)	1.50	☐
1984, 10 APRIL	PHQ74 URBAN RENEWAL (4)	1.25	☐
1984, 15 MAY	PHQ75 EUROPA (4)	1.25	☐
1984, 5 JUNE	PHQ76 THE ECONOMIC SUMMIT (1)	0.30	☐
1984, 26 JUNE	PHQ77 THE GREENWICH MERIDIAN (4)	1.50	☐
1984, 31 JULY	PHQ78 THE ROYAL MAIL (5)	1.50	☐
1984, 25 SEPTEMBER	PHQ79 THE BRITISH COUNCIL (4)	1.50	☐
1984, 20 NOVEMBER	PHQ80 CHRISTMAS (5)	1.50	☐
1985, 22 JANUARY	PHQ81 FAMOUS TRAINS (5)	1.75	☐
1985, 5 MARCH	PHQ82 INSECTS (5)	1.50	☐
1985, 14 MAY	PHQ83 MUSIC — COMPOSERS (4)	1.25	☐
1985, 18 JUNE	PHQ84 SAFETY AT SEA (4)	1.25	☐
1985, 30 JULY	PHQ85 ROYAL MAIL — 350th ANNIVERSARY OF THE POST OFFICE (4)	1.25	☐
1985, 3 SEPTEMBER	PHQ86 THE ARTHURIAN LEGEND (4)	1.25	☐
1985, 8 OCTOBER	PHQ87 BRITISH FILM YEAR (5)	1.50	☐
1985, 19 NOVEMBER	PHQ88 CHRISTMAS (5)	1.50	☐
1986, 18 FEBRUARY	PHQ90 REAPPEARANCE OF HALLEY'S COMET (4)	1.25	☐

		Price Perfect	Price Slight Fault
1986, 21 APRIL	PHQ91 60th BIRTHDAY OF HER MAJESTY QUEEN ELIZABETH II (2)...	1.25	☐
1986, 20 MAY	PHQ92 NATURE CONSERVATION (4).....................	1.25	☐
1986, 17 JUNE	PHQ93 900th ANNIVERSARY OF THE DOMESDAY BOOK (4)	1.25	☐
1986, 15 JULY	PHQ84 SPORT (5)...	1.50	☐
1986, 22 JULY	PHQ95 ROYAL WEDDING (2).............................	0.75	☐
1986, 19 SEPTEMBER	PHQ96 COMMONWEALTH PARLIAMENTARY CONFERENCE (1)..	0.30	☐
1986, 16 SEPTEMBER	PHQ97 RAF (5)...	1.50	☐
1986, 18 NOVEMBER	PHQ98 CHRISTMAS CUSTOMS (5).......................	1.50	☐

B) PHQ CARDS USED ON FIRST DAY OF ISSUE

This is a much more complicated aspect of PHQ Card collecting. In addition to the various possibilities of Special Postmarks, Philatelic Bureau Postmarks, First Day of Issue Town Postmarks or Local CDS's. We also have the complication of Used on the Face (obverse) or Used on the Reverse (back of the card). In addition some collectors like Gutter Pairs on PHQ Cards and Miniature Sheets have been affixed to others. In general, the best cards to collect are those with Connected or Pictorial Postmarks, either on the Face or Reverse depending on which way you prefer to collect them, in good condition. One has to bear in mind that PHQ Cards used on the First Day are Postal Items and, as such, can never be in the same condition as perfect Mint Cards. There is also the fact to remember that there are very very few of the early cards used on First Day and therefore tolerance is the key. The basic rule goes, as with all collecting, the better the condition the more pleasure it will give and the more likelihood it will hold its value.

As far as Special Postmarks are concerned, we have tried in a very small way to give an indication of the price premium for certain Postmarks. With sets of four of course there are enormous possibilities for different Postmarks. There is also the fact that collectors prefer different things. I personally prefer a set of four with four different Postmarks, preferably connected whereas on the Continent I gather they prefer four Philatelic Bureau Postmarks – I believe this is because they do not understand our Postmarks, they think the Philatelic Bureau is the only genuine one. If you are collecting New Issues I would strongly recommend you ensure that you get Special Postmarks. Under no circumstances collect your local FDI on PHQ Cards unless you particularly want it for a local collection as they will have little interest or value at a later date.

Face Reverse

PHQ1 **JULY 1973 CENTENARY OF COUNTY CRICKET** (1) 20,000

There was a story in 1973 that the man who invented the Pictorial Post Card, PHQ, died before his idea could come into general use. Nobody in the Post Office seemed to understand why they had been issued. In fact, I was told in 1973 that they were not issued for stamp collectors!!! When I asked what they were actually issued for there seemed to be some doubt as to what the reply should be. Because of this uncertainty the Cricket Card was never made available for the First Day of Issue of the cricket stamps on the 16th May. It was, in fact, released some time in July. There are two Cricket Postmarks during the summer of 1973 – one for the Benson & Hedges Cup and one for the Gilette Cup and either of these are acceptable as is any other date from July onwards. Some collectors I know collect the forged 16th May Postmarks. Obviously, these have a value but it must be remembered that they are back.dated by favour and under no circumstances can they be considered proper First Day of Issue Cards.

		Face	Reverse		
PHQ1a	Used with Benson & Hedges Postmark..............................	150.00	130.00	☐	☐
PHQ1b	Used with Gilette Cup Pictorial Postmark	140.00	120.00	☐	☐
PHQ1c	Used with any 1973 July or August date..........................	120.00	100.00	☐	☐
PHQ1d	Used with Forged FDI...	60.00	50.00	☐	☐

PHQ2 **15 AUGUST 1973 INIGO JONES** (1) 20,000

PHQ2a	Newmarket Special Pictorial Postmark...........................	125.00	100.00	☐	☐
PHQ2b	Wilton Special Postmark	120.00	95.00	☐	☐
PHQ2c	Bureau Special Postmark	110.00	80.00	☐	☐
PHQ2d	London WC FDI Handstamp	90.00	70.00	☐	☐
PHQ2e	Other FDI..	65.00	60.00	☐	☐
PHQ2d	Other Postmarks..	50.00	40.00	☐	☐

PHQ3 **12 SEPTEMBER 1973 PARLIAMENTARY CONFERENCE** (1) 15,200

PHQ3a	London SW1 Special Handstamp (Big Ben)	150.00	125.00	☐	☐
PHQ3b	Philatelic Bureau (House of Commons)...........................	140.00	115.00	☐	☐
PHQ3c	FDI...	90.00	80.00	☐	☐
PHQ3d	Other Postmarks..	80.00	70.00	☐	☐
PHQ3e	House of Commons CDS OR House of Lords CDS .... from	200.00	150.00	☐	☐

PHQ4 **14 NOVEMBER 1974 ROYAL WEDDING** (1) 190,000

PHQ4a	Great Somerfield OR Dragoon Guards postmark	40.00	30.00	☐	☐
PHQ4b	Westminster Abbey OR Windsor Postmark	35.00	25.00	☐	☐
PHQ4c	Philatelic Bureau	30.00	20.00	☐	☐
PHQ4d	FDI Any Town..	15.00	12.50	☐	☐
PHQ4e	Other Postmarks..	9.00	6.00	☐	☐
PHQ4f	Buckingham Palace OR Windsor Castle CDS Postmarks....... from	100.00	75.00	☐	☐

PHQ5 **27 FEBRUARY 1974 BRITISH TREES** (1) 16,750

PHQ5a	Stampex...	100.00	80.00	☐	☐
PHQ5b	Bureau	90.00	75.00	☐	☐
PHQ5c	FDI..	50.00	40.00	☐	☐
PHQ5d	Other..	40.00	35.00	☐	☐

PHQ6 **24 APRIL 1974 FIRE SERVICE ANNIVERSARY** (1) 30,000

PHQ6a	Sunderland..	100.00	85.00	☐	☐
PHQ6b	Cambridge OR Avon County Bristol	90.00	80.00	☐	☐
PHQ6c	Lancing Bagnall	110.00	90.00	☐	☐
PHQ6d	Philatelic Bureau	80.00	60.00	☐	☐
PHQ6e	FDI...	35.00	30.00	☐	☐
PHQ6f	Other Postmarks..	25.00	20.00	☐	☐

PHQ7 **10 JULY 1974 MEDIEVAL WARRIORS** (4) 31,750

PHQ7a	Set of four cards with Pictorial or connected Postmarks............	60.00	50.00	☐	☐
PHQ7b	Set of four cards with Philatelic Bureau Postmarks.................	50.00	40.00	☐	☐
PHQ7c	Set of four cards with FDI Postmarks	30.00	35.00	☐	☐
PHQ7d	Set of four cards wqith Other Postmarks..........................	20.00	15.00	☐	☐

PHQ8 **9 OCTOBER 1974 WINSTON CHURCHILL** (1) 114,434

PHQ8a	Somerset House OR BFPO 1874	30.00	25.00	☐	☐
PHQ8b	Oldham OR Woodford Green......................................	25.00	20.00	☐	☐
PHQ8c	Blenheim OR House of Commons Pictorial Postmark	20.00	15.00	☐	☐
PHQ8d	Philatelic Bureau	17.50	12.50	☐	☐
PHQ8e	House of Commons OR House of Lords CDS................. from	40.00	30.00	☐	☐
PHQ8f	FDI...	7.50	5.00	☐	☐
PHQ8g	Other Postmarks..	4.00	3.00	☐	☐

		Face	Reverse	
PHQ9	**19 FEBRUARY 1975 TURNER BICENTENARY** (1) 46,250			
PHQ9a	Harwich CDS, the site of the actual snowstorm	35.00	25.00	☐ ☐
PHQ9b	Philatelic Bureau OR London Special Postmark	17.50	15.00	☐ ☐
PHQ9c	FDI	8.00	6.00	☐ ☐
PHQ9d	Other Postmarks	6.00	4.00	☐ ☐
PHQ10	**23 APRIL 1975 EUROPEAN ARCHITECTURAL YEAR 1**(3) 51,000			
PHQ10a	Complete set with Pictorial or Relevant Postmarks	35.00	25.00	☐ ☐
PHQ10b	Complete set Philatelic Bureau Postmark	30.00	20.00	☐ ☐
PHQ10c	Complete set with FDI Postmark	12.00	10.00	☐ ☐
PHQ11	**11 JUNE 1975 SAILING** (1) 41,350			
PHQ11a	Royal Dorset OR Royal Thames Yacht Club	20.00	15.00	☐ ☐
PHQ11b	Philatelic Bureau	15.00	12.00	☐ ☐
PHQ11c	FDI	8.00	6.00	☐ ☐
PHQ11d	Other Postmarks	6.00	4.00	☐ ☐
PHQ12	**13 AUGUST 1975 150th ANNIVERSARY STOCKTON & DARLINGTON RAILWAY** (4) 47,500			
PHQ12a	Set with four Pictorial postmarks	70.00	45.00	☐ ☐
PHQ12b	Set with Philatelic Bureau Postmark	50.00	40.00	☐ ☐
PHQ12c	Set with FDI Postmark	25.00	20.00	☐ ☐
PHQ12d	Set with Other Postmarks	15.00	12.50	☐ ☐
PHQ13	**22 OCTOBER 1975 JANE AUSTEN BICENTENARY** (4) 27,337			
PHQ13a	Set of four Pictorial Postmarks	30.00	20.00	☐ ☐
PHQ13b	Set of four Philatelic Bureau Postmark	25.00	17.50	☐ ☐
PHQ13c	Set of four FDI Postmark	12.00	10.00	☐ ☐
PHQ13d	Set of four Other Postmarks	8.00	6.00	
PHQ14	**28 APRIL 1976 SOCIAL REFROMERS** (1) 38,350			
PHQ14as	Colliery CDS Postmark	25.00	20.00	☐ ☐
PHQ14b	Philatelic Bureau – Folkestone or Durham Postmarks	15.00	10.00	☐ ☐
PHQ14c	FDI Postmark	5.00	4.00	☐ ☐
PHQ14d	Other Postmarks	3.00	2.00	☐ ☐
PHQ15	**2 JUNE 1976 AMERICAN BICENTENARY** (1) 60,950			
PHQ15a	BFPS 1776 OR Greenwich 1776 Exhibition	20.00	15.00	☐ ☐
PHQ15b	Bath American Museum Plymouth Congress	17.50	15.00	☐ ☐
PHQ15c	Washington Tyne and Wear	15.00	12.50	☐ ☐
PHQ15d	Philatelic Bureau	13.00	11.00	☐ ☐
PHQ15e	FDI	8.00	6.00	
PHQ16	**30 JUNE 1976 ROSE SOCIETY CENTENARY** (4) 34,250			
PHQ16a	Set of four with Pictorial Postmarks	25.00	20.00	☐ ☐
PHQ16b	Set of four with Philatelic Bureau Postmark	20.00	15.00	☐ ☐
PHQ16c	Set of four with FDI Postmark	9.00	8.00	☐ ☐
PHQ17	**4 AUGUST 1976 BRITISH CULTURAL TRADITIONS** (4) 33,000			
PHQ17a	Set of four with Pictorial Postmarks	18.00	12.50	☐ ☐
PHQ17b	Set of four with Philatelic Bureau Postmark	16.00	11.00	☐ ☐
PHQ17c	Set of four with FDI Postmark	8.00	6.00	☐ ☐
PHQ18	**29 SEPTEMBER 1976 500th ANNIVERSARY OF BRITISH PRINTING** (4) 29,550			
PHQ18a	Set of four with Pictorial Postmarks	18.00	12.50	☐ ☐
PHQ18b	Set of four with Philatelic Bureau Postmark	16.00	11.00	☐ ☐
PHQ18c	Set of four with FDI Postmark	8.00	6.00	☐ ☐
N.B.	The caption on PHQ18 8½p incorrectly states the woodcut is of the Knight when in fact it is a woodcut of the Squire.			
PHQ19	**24 NOVEMBER 1976 CHRISTMAS** (4) 100,000			
PHQ19a	Set of four with Pictorial Postmarks	14.00	10.00	☐ ☐
PHQ19b	Set of four with Philatelic Bureau Postmark	12.00	8.00	☐ ☐
PHQ19c	Set of four with FDI Postmark	5.00	4.00	☐ ☐
PHQ20	**12 JANUARY 1977 RACKET SPORT** (4) 43,000			
PHQ20a	Set of four with Pictorial Postmarks	15.00	12.50	☐ ☐
PHQ20b	Set of four with Philatelic Bureau Postmark	12.50	10.00	☐ ☐
PHQ20c	Set of four with FDI Postmark	7.50	6.00	☐ ☐
PHQ21	**2 MARCH 1977 ROYAL INSTITUTE OF CHEMISTRY CENTENARY** (4) 51,400			
PHQ21a	Set of four with Pictorial Postmarks	15.00	12.50	☐ ☐
PHQ21b	Set of four with Philatelic Bureau Postmark	12.50	10.00	☐ ☐
PHQ21c	Set of four with FDI Postmark	7.50	6.00	☐ ☐

STAMPS

The Magazine for Discerning Philatelists

G.B. Round-Up – News, views & reviews

Auction Action – All the news from recent sales

Make Collecting Pay – A monthly guide to making the most of your hobby

New Issues – This month's releases

Crown Agents News – A regular bulletin of Commonwealth new issues

GB, Foreign & Commonwealth – Features on both collecting & Postal History

If you would like to see a recent copy of **STAMPS**, free of charge please write to:-

STAMPS
Marketing Dept.,
Bushfield House,
Orton Centre,
Peterborough,
PE2 0UW

		Face	Reverse		

PHQ22 — **11 MAY 1977 SILVER JUBILEE** (4) 100,000
- PHQ22a Set of four with Pictorial Postmarks .... 15.00 12.50 ☐ ☐
- PHQ22b Set of four with Philatelic Bureau Postmark ... 12.50 10.00 ☐ ☐
- PHQ22c Set of four with FDI Postmark .... 7.50   5.00   ☐ ☐

PHQ22E — **15 JUNE 1977 SILVER JUBILEE** (1) 100,000
- PHQ22Ea Pictorial Postmark .... 2.50   1.50   ☐ ☐
- PHQ22Eb Philatelic Bureau Postmark .... 2.00   1.00   ☐ ☐
- PHQ22Ec FDI Postmark 0.75   0.50

N.B. The number PHQ24 was originally set aside for the 9p Silver Jubilee Card issued after the rest of the set but the 9p Silver Jubilee Card was numbered PHQ22(e) and the Wildlife Set of Cards had then already been allocated PHQ25.

Any postmarks with Royalty connection such as Buckingham Palace or Windsor Castle will command a premium. Cards also known with Special Slogans are worth somewhere in the region of £5 premium.

PHQ23 — **8 JUNE 1977 HEADS OF GOVERNMENT** (1) 39,600
- PHQ23a London SW1 FDI Handstamp .... 5.00   4.00   ☐ ☐
- PHQ23b Philatelic Bureau Postmark .... 4.00   3.00   ☐ ☐
- PHQ23c FDI Postmark .... 2.00   1.50   ☐ ☐
- PHQ23d House of Lords OR House of Commons CDS ..from 15.00 10.00 ☐ ☐
- PHQ23e House of Commons Machine Slogan .... 10.00 7.50   ☐ ☐

PHQ24 — **NOT ISSUED** – See PHQ22E

PHQ25 — **5 OCTOBER 1977 BRITISH WILDLIFE** (5) 91,000 plus
- PHQ25a Set of five with Pictorial postmarks .... 7.50   5.00   ☐ ☐
- PHQ25b Set of five with Philatelic Bureau Postmark ... 6.00   4.00   ☐ ☐
- PHQ25c Set of five with FDI Postmark .... 2.50   2.00   ☐ ☐

PHQ26 — **23 NOVEMBER 1977 CHRISTMAS** (6) 120,000
- PHQ26a Set of six with Pictorial Postmarks .... 6.00   4.50   ☐ ☐
- PHQ26b Set of six with Philatelic Bureau Postmark .... 5.00   4.00   ☐ ☐
- PHQ26c Set of six with FDI Postmark .... 2.50   2.00   ☐ ☐

PHQ27 — **25 JANUARY 1978 ENERGY** (4) 80,000
- PHQ27a Set of four with Pictorial Postmarks .... 6.00   4.50   ☐ ☐
- PHQ27b Set of four with Philatelic Bureau Postmarks .. 5.00   4.00   ☐ ☐
- PHQ27c Set of four with FDI Postmark .... 2.50   2.00   ☐ ☐

PHQ28 — **1 MARCH 1978 BRITISH ARCHITECTURE HISTORIC BUILDINGS** (4) 85,000
- PHQ28a Set of four with Pictorial Postmarks .... 6.00   4.50   ☐ ☐
- PHQ28b Set of four with Philatelic Bureau Postmarks .. 5.00   4.00   ☐ ☐
- PHQ28c Set of four with FDI Postmark .... 2.50   2.00   ☐ ☐

PHQ29 — **31 MAY 1978 ANNIVERSARY OF THE CORONATION** (4) 125,000
- PHQ29a Set of four with Pictorial Postmarks .... 6.00   4.50   ☐ ☐
- PHQ29b Set of four with Philatelic Bureau Postmark ... 5.00   4.00   ☐ ☐
- PHQ29c Set of four with FDI Postmark .... 2.50   2.00   ☐ ☐

PHQ30 — **5 JULY 1978 SHIRE HORSE SOCIETY CENTENARY** (4) 200,000
- PHQ30a Set of four with Pictorial Postmarks .... 6.00   4.00   ☐ ☐
- PHQ30b Set of four with Philatelic Bureau Postmark ... 5.00   4.00   ☐ ☐
- PHQ30c Set of four with FDI Postmark .... 2.50   2.00   ☐ ☐

PHQ31 — **2 AUGUST 1978 CYCLING CENTENARIES** (4) 150,000
- PHQ31a Set of four with Pictorial Postmarks .... 4.50   3.50   ☐ ☐
- PHQ31b Set of four with Philatelic Bureau Postmark ... 3.00   2.50   ☐ ☐
- PHQ31c Set of four with FDI Postmark .... 1.50   1.00   ☐ ☐

PHQ32 — **22 NOVEMBER 1978 CHRISTMAS** (4) 170,000
- PHQ32a Set of four with Pictorial Postmarks .... 4.50   3.50   ☐ ☐
- PHQ32b Set of four with Philatelic Bureau Postmark ... 3.00   2.50   ☐ ☐
- PHQ32c Set of four with FDI Postmark .... 1.50   1.00   ☐ ☐

PHQ33 — **7 FEBRUARY 1979 BRITISH DOGS** (4) 180,000
- PHQ33a Set of four with Pictorial Postmarks .... 6.00   4.50   ☐ ☐
- PHQ33b Set of four with Philatelic Bureau Postmark ... 5.00   4.00   ☐ ☐
- PHQ33c Set of four with FDI Postmark .... 1.50   1.00   ☐ ☐

PHQ34 — **21 MARCH 1979 BRITISH FLOWERS** (4) 200,000
- PHQ34a Set of four with Pictorial Postmarks .... 4.50   3.50   ☐ ☐
- PHQ34b Set of four with Philatelic Bureau Postmark ... 4.00   3.00   ☐ ☐
- PHQ34c Set of four with FDI Postmark .... 2.00   1.50   ☐ ☐

PHQ47

PHQ59

   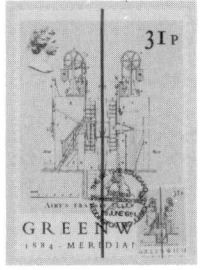

PHQ77

PHQ16

			Face	Reverse	
PHQ35	**9 MAY 1979 EUROPEAN ELECTIONS** (4) 160,000				
PHQ35a	Set of four with Pictorial Postmarks	3.50	2.75	☐ ☐
PHQ35b	Set of four with Philatelic Bureau Postmark	3.00	2.25	☐ ☐
PHQ35c	Set of four with FDI Postmark	1.50	1.00	☐ ☐
PHQ36	**6 JUNE 1979 HORSE RACING PAINTINGS** (4) 200,000				
PHQ36a	Set of four with Pictorial Postmarks	3.50	2.75	☐ ☐
PHQ36b	Set of four with Philatelic Bureau Postmark	3.00	2.25	☐ ☐
PHQ36c	Set of four with FDI Postmark	1.50	1.00	☐ ☐
PHQ37	**11 JULY 1979 INTERNATIONAL YEAR OF THE CHILD** (4) 250,000				
PHQ37a	Set of four with Pictorial Postmarks	4.50	3.00	☐ ☐
PHQ37b	Set of four with Philatelic Bureau Postmark	3.50	2.50	☐ ☐
PHQ29c	Set of four with FDI Postmark	1.00	1.00	☐ ☐
PHQ38	**22 AUGUST 1979 SIR ROWLAND HILL CENTENARY** (4) 250,000				
PHQ38a	Set of four with Pictorial Postmarks	3.50	3.00	☐ ☐
PHQ38b	Set of four with Philatelic Bureau Postmark	2.50	1.50	☐ ☐
PHQ38c	Set of four with FDI Postmark	1.00	1.00	☐ ☐

N.B. The PHQ38 10p cards also exist with a completely different reverse which states "With the Compliments of the British Post Office" in both English and French. This card was produced for the 1979 UPU Congress in Brazil. The matching 10p stamp is affixed to the picture side of the card and cancelled by a Special Handstamp. London EC1 UPU Day, 9th October '79. Price £100.00.

PHQ38d	24 OCTOBER 1979 Complete set with Miniature Sheet only available on reverse for obvious reasons.			
	Special postmark		12.00	☐
	FDI		6.00	☐
PHQ39	**26 SEPTEMBER 1979 150th ANNIVERSARY OF THE METROPOLITAN POLICE** (4) 250,000				
PHQ39a	Set of four with Pictorial Postmarks	3.50	3.00	☐ ☐
PHQ39b	Set of four with Philatelic Bureau Postmark	2.50	1.50	☐ ☐
PHQ39c	Set of four with FDI Postmark	1.00	1.00	☐ ☐
PHQ40	**21 NOVEMBER 1979 CHRISTMAS** (5) 250,000				
PHQ29a	Set of four with Pictorial Postmarks	6.00	4.50	☐ ☐
PHQ29b	Set of four with Philatelic Bureau Postmark	5.00	4.00	☐ ☐
PHQ29c	Set of four with FDI Postmark	2.50	2.00	☐ ☐
PHQ40a	Set of four with Pictorial Postmarks	3.50	2.50	☐ ☐
PHQ40b	Set of four with Philatelic Bureau Postmark	3.00	2.00	☐ ☐
PHQ40c	Set of four with FDI Postmark	1.00	1.00	☐ ☐
PHQ41	**16 JANUARY 1980 WILD BIRD PROTECTION ACT CENTENARY** (4) 260,000				
PHQ41a	Set of four with Pictorial Postmarks	4.00	3.00	☐ ☐
PHQ41b	Set of four with Philatelic Bureau Postmark	3.00	2.00	☐ ☐
PHQ41c	Set of four with FDI Postmark	1.00	1.00	☐ ☐
PHQ42	**12 MARCH 1980 LIVERPOOL AND MANCHESTER RAILWAY 150th ANNIVERSARY** (5) 265,000				
PHQ42a	Set of five with Pictorial Postmarks	4.50	3.00	☐ ☐
PHQ42b	Set of five with Philatelic Bureau Postmark	3.50	2.00	☐ ☐
PHQ42c	Set of five with FDI Postmark	1.50	1.50	☐ ☐
PHQ43	**9 APRIL 1980 LONDON 1980** (1) 300,000				
PHQ43a	London Pictorial Postmark	2.50	1.50	☐ ☐
PHQ43b	With Philatelic Bureau Postmark	1.50	1.00	☐ ☐
PHQ43c	With FDI Postmark	0.75	0.75	☐ ☐
PHQ43d	7 MAY 1980 Miniature Sheet Affixed. Reverse Only		2.00	☐
PHQ43	**7 MAY 1980 LONDON LANDMARKS** (5) 300,000				
PHQ43a	Set of five with Pictorial Postmarks	4.00	3.00	☐ ☐
PHQ43b	Set of five with Philatelic Bureau Postmark	3.00	2.00	☐ ☐
PHQ43c	Set of five with FDI Postmark	1.50	1.25	☐ ☐

N.B. It should be noted that the last two issues are both coded PHQ43.

PHQ44	**9 JULY 1980 FAMOUS AUTHORESSES** (5) 220,000				
PHQ44a	Set of five with Pictorial Postmarks	4.00	3.00	☐ ☐
PHQ44b	Set of five with Philatelic Bureau Postmark	3.00	2.00	☐ ☐
PHQ44c	Set of five with FDI Postmark	1.00	1.00	

DO YOU KNOW
THAT
VERA TRINDER LTD.
(INCORPORATING HARRIS PUBLICATIONS)

HAVE OVER 35 DIFFERENT FIRST DAY COVER ALBUMS AND 20 DIFFERENT POST CARD ALBUMS* IN STOCK

Our 32 pp. price list includes stockbooks, accessories, catalogues of all countries, UV lamps, magnifiers, plus the complete range of Gibbons, Godden, Prangnell-Rapkin. Illustrated brochures of Lighthouse, Ka-Be, Safe, Lindner etc.

Send for list to

VERA TRINDER LTD.
38 Bedford Street, London, WC2E 9EU.

*Including those made with the "Safe" material guaranteed not to harm your covers.

		Face	Reverse	
PHQ45	**4 AUGUST 1980 QUEEN MOTHER'S 80th BIRTHDAY** (1) 406,000			
PHQ45a	With Pictorial Postmark	2.00	1.50	☐ ☐
PHQ45b	With Pictorial Bureau Postmark	1.50	1.00	☐ ☐
PHQ45c	With FDI Postmark	0.75	0.75	☐ ☐
PHQ46	**10 SEPTEMBER 1980 BRITISH CONDUCTORS** (4) 225,000			
PHQ46a	Set of four with Pictorial Postmarks	3.00	2.50	☐ ☐
PHQ46b	Set of four with Philatelic Bureau Postmark	2.50	2.00	☐ ☐
PHQ46c	Set of four with FDI Postmark	1.25	1.00	☐ ☐
PHQ47	**10 OCTOBER 1980 SPORTS CENTENARIES** (4) 250,000			
PHQ47a	Set of four with Pictorial Postmarks	3.00	2.50	☐ ☐
PHQ47b	Set of four with Philatelic Bureau Postmark	2.50	2.00	☐ ☐
PHQ47c	Set of four with FDI Postmark	1.25	1.00	
N.B.	The Post Office's National Postal Museum overprinted a small number of the 12p card for their Exhibition of Elizabethan Sports Stamps and sold these cards with the 12p Sports Stamp affixed to the reverse For subsequent Exhibitions held at the Museum they have produced their own cards. FDI Special H/S price £10, Mint price £5.			
PHQ48	**19 NOVEMBER 1980 CHRISTMAS** (5) 250,000			
PHQ48a	Set of five with Pictorial Postmarks	3.00	2.50	☐ ☐
PHQ48b	Set of five with Philatelic Bureau Postmark	2.50	2.00	☐ ☐
PHQ48c	Set of five with FDI Postmark	1.25	1.00	☐ ☐
PHQ49	**6 FEBRUARY 1981 FOLKLORE** (4) 225,000			
PHQ49a	Set of four with Pictorial Postmarks	3.00	2.50	☐ ☐
PHQ49b	Set of four with Philatelic Bureau Postmark	2.50	2.00	☐ ☐
PHQ49c	set of four with FDI Postmark	1.25	1.00	☐ ☐
PHQ50	**25 MARCH 1981 INTERNATIONAL YEAR OF THE DISABLED** (4) 225,000			
PHQ50a	Set of four with Pictorial Postmarks	3.00	2.50	☐ ☐
PHQ50b	Set of four with Philatelic Bureau Postmark	2.50	2.00	☐ ☐
PHQ50c	Set of four with FDI Postmark	1.25	1.00	☐ ☐

FOR
GOOD EARLY COVERS
OR UNUSUAL POSTMARKS
TRY

BREDON HILL STAMPS

COVER AUCTIONS

POSTAL BID SALES ARE HELD EVERY SIX WEEKS APPROX.

SAMPLE CATALOGUE SENT FREE ON REQUEST
(Annual Subscription £4.00)

IS YOUR COLLECTION ADEQUATELY INSURED?
For just £15* per year, you could have peace of mind for a collection valued at £3000.
Full details and Proposal Form from us.
*rates may vary according to area

BREDON HILL STAMPS
ASHTON UNDER HILL, EVESHAM, WORCS, WR11 6TB. TEL (0386) 881374

			Face	Reverse	
PHQ51	**13 MAY 1981 BUTTERFLIES** (4) 250,000				
PHQ51	Set of four with Pictorial Postmark		4.00	3.00	☐ ☐
PHQ51b	Set of four with Philatelic Bureau Postmark		3.00	2.00	☐ ☐
PHQ51c	Set of four with FDI Postmark		1.50	1.25	☐ ☐
PHQ52	**24 JUNE 1981 NATIONAL TRUSTS** (5) 203,000				
PHQ52a	Set of five with Pictorial Postmarks		3.50	3.00	☐ ☐
PHQ52b	Set of five with Philatelic Bureau Postmark		3.00	2.50	☐ ☐
PHQ52c	Set of five with FDI Postmark		1.50	1.25	
PHQ53	**22 JULY 1981 Royal Wedding** (2) 760,000				
PHQ53a	Set of two with Pictorial Postmarks		3.00	2.50	☐ ☐
PHQ53b	Set of two with Philatelic Bureau Postmark		2.50	2.00	☐ ☐
PHQ53c	Set of two with FDI Postmark		1.50	1.25	☐ ☐
PHQ54	**12 AUGUST 1981 DUKE OF EDINBURGH'S AWARD** (4) 257,000				
PHQ54a	Set of four with Pictorial Postmarks		3.00	2.00	☐ ☐
PHQ54b	Set of four with Philatelic Bureau Postmark		2.50	1.50	☐ ☐
PHQ54c	Set of four with FDI Postmark		1.00	1.00	☐ ☐
PHQ55	**23 SEPTEMBER 1981 FISHING** (4) 270,000				
PHQ55a	Set of four with Pictorial Postmarks		3.00	2.00	☐ ☐
PHQ55b	Set of four with Philatelic Bureau Postmark		2.50	1.50	☐ ☐
PHQ55c	Set of four with FDI Postmark		1.00	1.00	
PHQ56	**18 NOVEMBER 1981 CHRISTMAS** (5) 294,000				
PHQ56a	Set of five with Pictorial Postmarks		3.50	2.50	☐ ☐
PHQ56b	Set of five with Philatelic Bureau Postmark		2.50	2.00	☐ ☐
PHQ56c	Set of five with FDI Postmark		1.25	1.25	☐ ☐
PHQ57	**10 FEBRUARY 1982 CHARLES DARWIN** (4) 241,000				
PHQ57a	Set of four with Pictorial Postmarks		3.00	2.50	☐ ☐
PHQ57b	Set of four with Philatelic Bureau Postmark		2.50	2.00	☐ ☐
PHQ57c	Set of four with FDI Postmark		1.25	1.25	☐ ☐
PHQ58	**24 MARCH 1982 YOUTH ORGANISATIONS** (4) 235,000				
PHQ58a	Set of four with Pictorial Postmarks		3.00	2.50	☐ ☐
PHQ58b	Set of four with Philatelic Bureau Postmark		2.50	2.00	☐ ☐
PHQ58c	Set of four with FDI Postmark		1.25	1.25	
PHQ59	**28 APRIL 1982 BRITISH THEATRE** (4) 233,000				
PHQ59a	Set of four with Pictorial Postmarks		3.00	2.50	☐ ☐
PHQ59b	Set of four with Philatelic Bureau Postmark		2.50	2.00	☐ ☐
PHQ59c	Set of four with FDI Postmark		1.25	1.25	☐ ☐
PHQ60	**16 JUNE 1982 MARITIME HERITAGE** (5) 252,000				
PHQ60a	Set of five with Pictorial Postmarks		6.00	4.50	☐ ☐
PHQ60b	Set of five with Philatelic Bureau Postmark		5.00	4.00	☐ ☐
PHQ60c	Set of five with FDI Postmark		2.00	1.50	☐ ☐
PHQ61	**23 JULY 1982 BRITISH TEXTILES** (4) 210,000				
PHQ61a	Set of four with Pictorial Postmarks		3.00	2.50	☐ ☐
PHQ61b	Set of four with Philatelic Bureau Postmark		2.50	2.00	☐ ☐
PHQ61c	Set of four with FDI Postmark		1.25	1.25	
PHQ62	**8 SEPTEMBER 1982 INFORMATION TECHNOLOGY YEAR** (2) 248,000				
PHQ62a	Set of two with Pictorial Postmarks		2.50	1.75	☐ ☐
PHQ62b	Set of two with Philatelic Bureau Postmark		2.00	1.75	☐ ☐
PHQ62c	Set of two with FDI Postmark		0.75	0.75	☐ ☐
PHQ63	**13 OCTOBER 1982 BRITISH MOTOR CARS** (4) 225,000				
PHQ63a	Set of four with Pictorial Postmarks		5.00	4.00	☐ ☐
PHQ63b	Set of four with Philatelic Bureau Postmark		4.00	3.00	☐ ☐
PHQ63c	Set of four with FDI Postmark		1.50	1.25	☐ ☐
N.B.	There is no need to write to the Post Office as they have already informed us that incorrect information is shown on the four PHQ Cards 63A, B, C and D. It attributes the stamp designs to Tayburn Design and Marketing Ltd. who were actually responsible for the First Day Cover, Presentation Pack and Philatelic Wallchart designs. Stanley Paine was the designer of the stamps.				
PHQ64	**17 NOVEMBER 1982 CHRISTMAS** (5) 231,000				
PHQ64a	Set of five with Pictorial Postmarks		4.50	3.75	☐ ☐
PHQ64b	Set of five with Philatelic Bureau Postmark		4.00	3.00	☐ ☐
PHQ64c	Set of five with FDI Postmarks		1.50	1.25	☐ ☐

			Face	Reverse		
PHQ65	**26 JANUARY 1983 FISH** (4) 195,000					
PHQ65a	Set of four with Pictorial Postmarks		4.00	3.00	☐	☐
PHQ65b	Set of four with Philatelic Bureau Postmark		3.50	2.50	☐	☐
PHQ65c	Set of four with FDI Postmark		1.50	1.25	☐	☐
PHQ66	**9 MARCH 1983 COMMONWEALTH DAY** (4) 189,000					
PHQ66a	Set of four with Pictorial Postmarks		4.00	3.00	☐	☐
PHQ66b	Set of four with Philatelic Bureau Postmark		3.50	2.50	☐	☐
PHQ66c	Set of four with FDI Postmark		1.50	1.25	☐	☐
PHQ67	**25 MAY 1983 ENGINEERING** (3) 197,000					
PHQ67a	Set of three with Pictorial Postmarks		3.00	2.50	☐	☐
PHQ67b	Set of three with Philatelic Bureau Postmark		2.50	2.25	☐	☐
PHQ67c	Set of three with FDI Postmark		1.25	1.00	☐	☐
PHQ68	**6 JULY 1983 BRITISH ARMY** (5) 195,000					
PHQ68a	Set of five with Pictorial Postmarks		6.00	4.50	☐	☐
PHQ68b	Set of five with Philatelic Bureau Postmark		5.00	3.50	☐	☐
PHQ68c	Set of five with FDI Postmark		1.75	1.50	☐	☐
PHQ69	**24 AUGUST 1983 GARDENS** (4)					
PHQ69a	Set of four with Pictorial Postmarks		3.50	3.00	☐	☐
PHQ69b	Set of four with Philatelic Bureau Postmark		3.00	2.50	☐	☐
PHQ69c	Set of four with FDI Postmark		1.50	1.25	☐	☐
PHQ70	**5 OCTOBER 1983 FAIRS** (4)					
PHQ70a	Set of four with Pictorial Postmarks		3.50	3.00	☐	☐
PHQ70b	Set of four with Philatelic Bureau Postmark		3.00	2.50	☐	☐
PHQ70c	Set of four with FDI Postmark		1.50	1.25	☐	☐
PHQ71	**16 NOVEMBER 1983 CHRISTMAS** (5)					
PHQ71a	Set of five with Pictorial Postmarks		5.00	4.00	☐	☐
PHQ71b	Set of five with Philatelic Bureau Postmark		4.00	3.00	☐	☐
PHQ71c	Set of five with FDI Postmark		1.75	1.50	☐	☐
PHQ72	**17 JANUARY 1984 HERALDRY** (4)					
PHQ72a	Set of four with Pictorial Postmarks		6.00	5.00	☐	☐
PHQ72b	Set of four with Philatelic Bureau Postmark		5.00	4.00	☐	☐
PHQ72c	Set of four with FDI Postmark		2.00	1.50	☐	☐
PHQ73	**6 MARCH 1984 CATTLE** (5)					
PHQ73a	Set of five with Pictorial Postmark		6.00	5.00	☐	☐
PHQ73b	Set of five with Philatelic Bureau Postmark		5.00	4.00	☐	☐
PHQ73c	Set of five with FDI Postmark		2.00	1.75	☐	☐
PHQ74	**10 APRIL 1984 URBAN RENEWAL** (4)					
PHQ74a	Set of four with Pictorial Postmark		5.00	3.50	☐	☐
PHQ74b	Set of four with Philatelic Bureau Postmark		4.00	3.00	☐	☐
PHQ74c	Set of four with FDI Postmark		1.50	1.50	☐	☐
PHQ75	**15 MAY 1984 EUROPA** (4)					
PHQ75a	Set of four with Pictorial Postmarks		5.00	3.50	☐	☐
PHQ75b	Set of four with Philatelic Bureau Postmark		4.00	3.00	☐	☐
PHQ75c	Set of four with FDI Postmark		1.50	1.50	☐	☐
PHQ76	**5 JUNE 1984 THE ECONOMIC SUMMIT** (1)					
PHQ76a	With Pictorial Postmark		2.00	1.50	☐	☐
PHQ76b	With Philatelic Bureau Postmark		1.50	1.25	☐	☐
PHQ76c	With FDI Postmark		0.75	0.50	☐	☐
PHQ77	**26 JUNE 1984 THE GREENWICH MERIDIAN** (4)					
PHQ77a	Set of four with Pictorial Postmarks		5.00	3.50	☐	☐
PHQ77b	Set of four with Philatelic Bureau Postmark		4.00	3.00	☐	☐
PHQ77c	Set of four with FDI Postmark		1.50	1.50	☐	☐
PHQ78	**31 JULY 1984 THE ROYAL MAIL** (5)					
PHQ78	Set of five with Pictorial Postmarks		6.00	5.00	☐	☐
PHQ78b	Set of five with Philatelic Bureau Postmark		5.00	4.00	☐	☐
PHQ78c	Set of five with FDI Postmark		2.00	1.75	☐	☐
PHQ79	**25 SEPTEMBER 1984 THE BRITISH COUNCIL** (4)					
PHQ79a	Set of four with Pictorial Postmarks		4.00	3.00	☐	☐
PHQ79b	Set of four with Philatelic Bureau Postmark		3.50	2.50	☐	☐
PHQ79c	Set of four with FDI Postmark		1.50	1.25	☐	☐

		Face	Reverse		
PHQ80	**20 NOVEMBER 1984 CHRISTMAS** (5)				
PHQ80a	Set of five with Pictorial Postmark	5.00	4.00	☐	☐
PHQ80b	Set of five with Philatelic Bureau Postmark	4.00	3.50	☐	☐
PHQ80c	Set of five with FDI Postmark	1.75	1.50	☐	☐
PHQ81	**22 JANUARY 1985 FAMOUS TRAINS** (5)				
PHQ81a	Set of five with Pictorial Postmark	10.00	7.50	☐	☐
PHQ81b	Set of five with Philatelic Bureau Postmark	6.00	5.00	☐	☐
PHQ81c	Set of five with FDI Postmark	2.50	2.00	☐	☐
PHQ82	**5 MARCH 1985 INSECTS** (5)				
PHQ82a	Set of five with Pictorial Postmarks	5.00	4.00	☐	☐
PHQ82b	Set of five with Philatelic Bureau Postmark	4.00	3.50	☐	☐
PHQ82c	Set of five with FDI Postmark	1.75	1.50	☐	☐
PHQ83	**14 MAY 1985 MUSIC – COMPOSERS** (4)				
PHQ83a	Set of four with Pictorial Postmarks	4.50	3.75	☐	☐
PHQ83b	Set of four with Philatelic Bureau Postmark	4.00	3.25	☐	☐
PHQ83c	Set of four with FDI Postmark	1.75	1.50	☐	☐
PHQ84	**18 JUNE 1985 SAFETY AT SEA** (4)				
PHQ84a	Set of four with Pictorial Postmarks	4.50	3.75	☐	☐
PHQ84b	Set of four with Philatelic Bureau Postmark	4.00	3.25	☐	☐
PHQ84c	Set of four with FDI Postmark	1.75	1.50	☐	☐
PHQ85	**30 JULY 1985 ROYAL MAIL – 350th ANNIVERSARY OF THE POST OFFICE** (4)				
PHQ85a	Set of four with Pictorial Postmarks	4.50	3.75	☐	☐
PHQ85b	Set of four with Philatelic Bureau Postmark	4.00	3.25	☐	☐
PHQ85c	Set of four with FDI Postmark	1.75	1.50	☐	☐
PHQ86	**3 SEPTEMBER 1985 THE ARTHURIAN LEGEND** (4)				
PHQ86a	Set of four with Pictorial Postmarks	4.50	3.75	☐	☐
PHQ86b	Set of four with Philatelic Bureau Postmark	4.00	3.25	☐	☐
PHQ86c	Set of four with FDI Postmark	1.75	1.50	☐	☐
PHQ87	**8 OCTOBER 1985 BRITISH FILM YEAR** (5)				
PHQ87a	Set of five with Pictorial Postmarks	6.00	5.00	☐	☐
PHQ87b	Set of five with Philatelic Bureau Postmark	4.50	4.00	☐	☐
PHQ87c	Set of five with FDI Postmark	2.00	1.75	☐	☐
PHQ88	**19 NOVEMBER 1985 CHRISTMAS** (5)				
PHQ88a	Set of five with Pictorial Postmarks	5.00	4.00	☐	☐
PHQ88b	Set of five with Philatelic Bureau Postmark	4.00	3.50	☐	☐
PHQ88c	Set of five with FDI Postmark	2.00	1.75	☐	☐
PHQ89	**14 JANUARY 1986 BRITISH INDUSTRY YEAR** (4)				
PHQ89a	Set of four with Pictorial Postmarks	4.50	4.00	☐	☐
PHQ89b	Set of four with Philatelic Bureau Postmark	4.00	3.50	☐	☐
PHQ89c	Set of four with FDI Postmark	2.00	1.50	☐	☐
PHQ90	**18 FEBRUARY 1986 REAPPEARANCE OF HALLEY'S COMET** (4)				
PHQ90a	Set of four with Pictorial Postmarks	4.50	4.00	☐	☐
PHQ90b	Set of four with Philatelic Bureau Postmark	4.00	3.50	☐	☐
PHQ90c	Set of four with FDI Postmark	2.00	1.50	☐	☐
PHQ91	**21 APRIL 1986 60th BIRTHDAY OF HER MAJESTY QUEEN ELIZABETH II** (2)				
PHQ91a	Set of two with Pictorial Postmarks	5.00	4.00	☐	☐
PHQ91b	Set of two with Philatelic Bureau Postmark	4.00	3.50	☐	☐
PHQ91c	Set of two with FDI Postmark	2.00	1.50	☐	☐
PHQ92	**20 MAY 1986 NATURE CONSERVATION/EUROPA** (4)				
PHQ92a	Set of four with Pictorial Postmarks	5.00	4.00	☐	☐
PHQ92b	Set of four with Philatelic Bureau Postmark	4.00	3.50	☐	☐
PHQ92c	Set of four with FDI Postmark	2.00	1.50	☐	☐
PHQ93	**17 JUNE 1986 900th ANNIVERSARY OF THE DOMESDAY BOOK** (4)				
PHQ93a	Set of four with Pictorial Postmarks	5.00	4.00	☐	☐
PHQ93b	Set of four with Philatelic Bureau Postmark	4.00	3.50	☐	☐
PHQ93c	Set of four with FDI Postmark	2.00	1.50	☐	☐
PHQ94	**15 JULY 1986 SPORT** (5)				
PHQ94	Set of five with Pictorial Postmarks	6.00	5.00	☐	☐
PHQ94b	Set of five with Philatelic Bureau Postmark	4.50	4.00	☐	☐
PHQ94c	Set of five with FDI Postmark	2.50	2.00	☐	☐

		Face	Reverse		
PHQ95	**22 JULY 1986 THE ROYAL WEDDING** (2)				
PHQ95a	Set of two with Pictorial Postmarks	3.00	2.00	☐	☐
PHQ95b	Set of two with Philatelic Bureau Postmark	2.00	1.50	☐	☐
PHQ95c	Set of two with FDI Postmark	1.00	1.00		
PHQ96	**19 AUGUST 1986 COMMONWEALTH PARLIAMENTARY CONFERENCE** (1)				
PHQ96a	With Pictorial Postmark	2.00	1.50	☐	☐
PHQ96b	With Philatelic Bureau Postmark	1.50	1.25	☐	☐
PHQ96c	With FDI Postmark	1.00	0.75	☐	☐
PHQ97	**16 SEPTEMBER 1986 R.A.F.** (5)				
PHQ97a	Set of five with Pictorial Postmarks	7.50	6.00	☐	☐
PHQ97b	Set of five with Philatelic Bureau Postmark	6.50	5.00	☐	☐
PHQ97c	Set of five with FDI Postmark	3.00	2.50	☐	☐
PHQ98	**18 NOVEMBER 1986 CHRISTMAS CUSTOMS** (5)				
PHQ98a	Set of five with Pictorial Postmarks	6.00	5.00	☐	☐
PHQ98b	Set of five with Philatelic Bureau Postmark	5.00	4.00	☐	☐
PHQ98c	Set of five with FDI Postmark	2.00	1.75	☐	☐
PHQ99	**2 DECEMBER 1986 CHRISTMAS CUSTOM 12p STAMP USED ON FACE ON PHQ98a** therefore creating a new PHQ Card. Only available on face.				
PHQ99a	With Pictorial Postmark	3.50		☐	
PHQ99b	With Philatelic Bureau Postmark	2.50		☐	
PHQ99c	With FDI Postmark	1.00		☐	

BUYING AT SOUTH LONDON

As we do not buy at auction, we urgently need to buy stamps, FDC, PHQ and collections, particularly GB.
—PLEASE VISIT OUR SHOP—
Late opening Friday up to 7pm

No. 1 NEW ISSUE SERVICE

 **SILKS**

Pres. Phil. Silks
PHQ and NPM Cards.
Please write for details.

 Sajal Philatelics

4 Amen Corner, Mitcham Road, London SW17.
Telephone: 01-672 6702   01-949 2771 (Evening)

SECTION II GUERNSEY

			FDI Special H/S	Mint		

1980, 7 MAY — **LONDON 1980**
An individual Jumbo size card was issued at the London 1980 Exhibition to which was affixed the 1980 Police and Europa sets of stamps and cancelled on the opening of the Exhibition. Price £4.00.

1980, 15 NOVEMBER — **PETER LE LIEVRE PAINTINGS**
Official Set No. 1   Set of 5 .... 4.00   1.50 ☐ ☐

1981, 22 MAY — **EUROPA**
A set of two cards was issued for the Europa 1981 stamps. These were not official postcards but so reproduce the two stamps exactly and were printed by the House of Questa by permission of the Guernsey Philatelic Bureau. They were distributed by Stamp Magazine. Price £2.25/£2.50 (FDI pmk) 75p/90p (Mint).

1981, 29 JULY — **ROYAL WEDDING**
Official Set No. 2   Set of 7 .... 4.00   1.50 ☐ ☐

1981, 28 APRIL — **LA SOCIETE GUERNESIASE EUROPA**
Official Set No. 3   Set of 6 .... 3.50   1.25 ☐ ☐

1983, 6 SEPTEMBER — **PAINTINGS – RENOIR**
Various paintings on 5 cards
Set of 5 .... 3.75   1.00 ☐ ☐

SECTION III JERSEY

			FDI Special H/S	Mint		

1979, 9 OCTOBER — **POST OFFICE HEADQUARTERS**
Set No. 1   40p Definitive .... 3.50   0.40 ☐ ☐

1981, 29 SEPTEMBER — **CHRISTMAS 1981**
Set No. 2   Set of 3 .... 1.75   0.50 ☐ ☐

1984, 1 JUNE — **LIFEBOATS**
Set No. 3   One card with single stamp .... 0.30 ☐
With full set of 6 stamps .... 3.50 ☐

1984, 21 SEPTEMBER — **LINKS WITH AUSTRALIA**
Set No. 4   Set with FDI .... 3.00   0.90 ☐ ☐

1985, — — — **LIBERATION**
Set No. 5   Set with FDI .... 1.25   0.90 ☐ ☐

DOUG & DAVE HARDY
9, BEXLEIGH GARDENS, ASPLEY,
NOTTINGHAM. TEL: 0602 298224

FOR REGIONAL CARDS, PHQ's
& FIRST DAY COVERS

ALSO G.B. COMMEMS. & DEFINS.
PRESENTATION PACKS & MACHINS
NEW ISSUE SERVICE AVAILABLE
DETAILS SENT ON REQUEST

We are also interested in buying any of
of the above subject to stock.

GREAT BRITAIN FIRST DAY COVERS
BENHAM "SILKS"   ★   REGIONAL POSTCARDS
NEW ISSUE SERVICE
P.H.Q. POSTCARDS   ★   AIR LETTERS
NEW ISSUE SERVICE
Good stocks of Covers, "Silks", Regional Postcards, P.H.Q. Postcards, Air Letters **OLD and NEW**.
NEW ISSUE SERVICE
We also stock G.B. stamps, booklets, cylinder blocks and Stamps for Commonwealth, Europe and the rest of the World.
NEW ISSUE SERVICE
For details of our New Issue Service and our current price lists write to:—

JOHN G. RICE STAMP CO.
"Kalahari" 1 Streetly Drive, Four Oaks, Sutton Coldfield B74 4PY

SECTION IV   ISLE OF MAN

		FDI Special H/S	Mint
1982, 1 JUNE Set No. 1	**75th ANNIVERSARY I.O.M. T.T. RACES** Complete set of 5..	2.50	1.00 ☐ ☐

N.B.   Chrstmas Cards have also been issued by the Isle of Man Post Office, these have a Christmas stamp affixed and are tied by an undated Christmas cachet.

1979 No. 1	**CHRISTMAS 1979** 7p Year of the Child...		0.75 ☐
1980 No. 2	**CHRISTMAS 1980** 8p Wildlife Conservation		0.75 ☐
1981 No. 3	**CHRISTMAS 1981** 9p Year of the Disabled		0.50 ☐
1982 No. 4	**CHRISTMAS 1982**		0.50 ☐
1983, 5 JULY Set No. 2	**10th ANNIVERSARY** I.O.M. set of 2 cards..	1.25	0.50 ☐ ☐
1983 No. 5	**CHRISTMAS 1983**		0.50 ☐
1984 No. 6	**CHRISTMAS 1984**		0.50 ☐
1985 No. 7	**CHRISTMAS 1985**		0.50 ☐
1986 No. 8	**CHRISTMAS 1986**		0.50 ☐

EXHIBITION CARDS

1982, 1 SEPTEMBER	SAN MARINO..	0.75	0.75 ☐ ☐
1982, 1 SEPTEMBER	SAN MARINO (with special cachet).......................	1.50	1.25 ☐ ☐
1983, 23 MAY	TEMBAL	0.75	0.75 ☐ ☐
1983, 23 MAY	TEMBAL (with Exhibition cachet)	1.50	1.25 ☐ ☐
1984, 27 APRIL	ESPANA	0.75	0.75 ☐ ☐
1984, 26 JUNE	BPE CONGRESS CARD....................................	2.00	0.50 ☐ ☐
1984, 21 SEPTEMBER	AUSIPEX...	0.75	0.75 ☐ ☐
1984, 21 SEPTEMBER	AUSIPEX (with Exhibiton cachet)	1.50	1.25 ☐ ☐
1985, No. 7	**MOTORING** (100 Years of the Car) Complete set of 5...	3.50	1.25 ☐ ☐

NEW ISSUE SERVICE
G.B. FIRST DAY COVERS
AND PHQ's

Special H/S, C.D.S. or Slogans
Definitive and Booklet F.D.C.'s
PHQ's Special H/S, front or back

Benham 'Silks' and Cards also supplied

FOR DETAILS, PHONE OR WRITE TO:

BERNARD CAMPLING (CF)

7 Oakleigh Gdns., Oldland Common,
Bristol BS15 6RJ. Tel: Bitton (0272) 322517

SPECIAL OFFERS
UNTIL 30th JUNE 1987
subject to stocks lasting

The following Benham 'Silk' F.D.I. Cards:-
Royal Wedding 1981 (2 cards) £25.00
1982 Year Set (33 cards)..................... £16.50
1983 Year Set (39 cards)..................... £19.50
1984 Year Set (36 cards)..................... £38.00
1985 Year Set (31 cards)..................... £40.00
1986 Year Set (39 cards)..................... £57.00
1982-1986 Year Sets complete............. £150.00
1986 Christmas 'Silk' Maxi Card (Benham)... £10.00
1987 New Issues. Per card postage free £1.50

S.P.D. STAMPS, Little Acre, Cheltenham
Road, Painswick, Glos GL6 6TS.
Tel. 0452-813641 *(weekends and evenings).*

SECTION V   BENHAM 'SILK' CARDS

These cards are issued for every Commemorative Set of Stamps from Great Britain. The 1982 Series had a standard border but from 1983 onwards the cards come in a mixture of borders to make them more attractive. From 1986 they are with interesting text on the reverse as shown with the illustrated set.

There are large numbers of 1982 available due to over-enthusiastic ordering by the trade but latter cards, particularly 1984 to 1986, are in short supply. The total number of cards produced from 1986 is limited to 2,500 including Mint.

		FDI	Mint		
FORERUNNER	1981 **ROYAL WEDDING,** FIRST DAY WITH ALTHORP AND LULLINGSTONE POSTMARKS	35.00	12.00	☐	☐

1982 SERIES
BPC.1	Darwin (4)	3.00	2.00	☐	☐
BPC.2	Youth (4)	3.00	2.00	☐	☐
BPC.3	Theatre (4)	3.00	2.00	☐	☐
BPC.4	Maritime (5)	6.00	2.50	☐	☐
BPC.5	Textiles (4)	3.00	2.00	☐	☐
BPC.6	Technology (2)	2.00	1.25	☐	☐
BPC.7	Cars (4)	7.50	2.50	☐	☐
BPC.8	Christmas (5)	4.00	2.25	☐	☐
	Year Set	27.00	15.00	☐	☐

1983 SERIES
BPC.1	River Fishes (4)	4.00	2.25	☐	☐
BPC.2	Commonwealth Day (4)	4.00	2.10	☐	☐
BPC.3	Engineering (3)	3.00	1.50	☐	☐
BPC.4	Military (4)	7.00	2.50	☐	☐
BPC.5	Gardens (4)	4.00	2.00	☐	☐
BPC.6	Fairs(4)	4.00	2.00	☐	☐
BPC.7	Christmas (5)	5.50	2.50	☐	☐
	Year Set	30.00	13.00	☐	☐

1984 SERIES
BPC.1	Heraldry (4)	10.00	3.50	☐	☐
BPC.2	Cattle (5)	6.50	2.50	☐	☐
BPC.3	Urban Renewal (4)	5.00	2.00	☐	☐
BPC.4	Europa (4)	5.00	2.00	☐	☐
BPC.5	The Economic Summit (1)	2.50	0.75	☐	☐
BPC.6	The Greenwich Meridian (4)	5.50	2.00	☐	☐

BPC.7	The Royal Mail (5)	10.00	2.50	☐	☐
BPC.8	The British Council (4)	5.00	2.00	☐	☐
BPC.9	Christmas (5)	6.00	2.50	☐	☐
	Year Set	50.00	18.00	☐	☐

1985 SERIES
BPC.1	Railway – Famous Trains (5)	12.50	2.50	☐	☐
BPC.2	Insects (5)	7.50	2.50	☐	☐
BPC.3	Music – Composers(4)	7.50	2.50	☐	☐
BPC.4	Safety at Sea (4)	6.00	2.50	☐	☐
BPC.5	Royal Mail – '350th Anniversary of The Post Office' (4)	6.00	2.50	☐	☐
BPC.6	The Arthurian Legend (4)	7.00	2.50	☐	☐
BPC.7	British Film Year (5)	7.50	2.50	☐	☐
BPC.8	Christmas (5)	7.00	2.50	☐	☐

1986 SERIES
BPC.1	Industry Year (4)	6.00	2.00	☐	☐
BPC.2	Halleys Comet (4)	7.00	2.50	☐	☐
BPC.3	Her Majesty the Queen 60th Birthday (4)	7.00	2.50	☐	☐
BPC.4	Europa (4) Conservation	7.50	4.00	☐	☐
BPC.5	Domesday Book (4)	7.50	2.50	☐	☐
BPC.6	Commonwealth Games (5)	7.50	2.50	☐	☐
BPC.7	Royal Wedding (2)	8.00	1.50	☐	☐
BPC.8	Parliamentary Association (1)	3.00	0.50	☐	☐
BPC.9	RAF (5)	10.00	2.50	☐	☐
BPC.10	Christmas (5) Christmas Customs	9.00	2.50	☐	☐

N.B. Benham have also produced many commorative cards with special postmarks. Details of these can be found in **COLLECT BENHAM COVERS 1987 EDITION £3.50** (including postage). All of the above cards are available from **Benham (A. Buckingham) Ltd.,** at the same prices. This is Benham's price list. Benham also run a new issue service for future issues.

 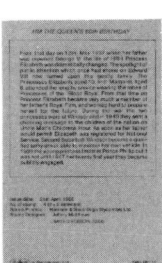  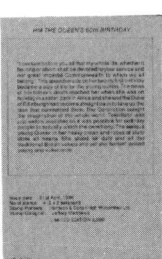

 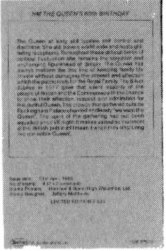  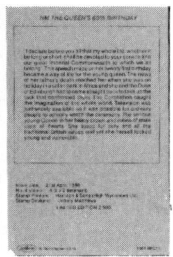

BPC.3   1986 Her Majesty the Queen's 60th Birthday – New Format Card.

REGIONAL CARDS

Regional cards are picture postcards published by the Post Office issued by the Regional Boards or by Head Postmasters for sale over post office counters in their own regions. Many regional issued cards have also been sold by the National Postal Museum and the British Philatelic Bureau, Edinburgh. The policy adopted in 1985 was to withdraw regional cards after a twelve month period of sale. The cards, issued singly or in sets, mostly depict subjects directly related to the issuing region and many have featured post office services such as 'The Post Bus', 'Postboxes', 'Rail and Air Transport of Mail'.

The earliest cards listed in the section are those sold at the Post Office Tower from May 1966 issued by the telecommunications division of the Post Office, London Region. The National Postal Museum first issued its own cards in November 1969. The first picture card to be issued by the Postal division of a Regional Board was that depicting the Dorchester PO Mural (in South Western Region) in October 1971. PHQ 'stamp' cards did not appear until 1973. The last cards to be issued by the Regional Boards were SEPR50, featuring Mobile Post Office GPO1 and SWPR29-32 RAF aircraft, all issued 30 September 1986.

CATALOGUE NUMBERING

Cards are listed and numbered in first date of sale order unless more practical to group otherwise. Where reprints have been issued and can be readily distinguished from the original printing the print number appears in brackets, e.g. SE2(2) Farnham PO Mural 2nd printing. The order in which they appear in the section and the prefixes used, are as follows:-

E	Eastern Postal Region	SW	South Western Postal Region
LT	London Post Office Tower	WM	Wales and the Marches Postal Region
L	London Postal Region	S	Scottish Postal Region
M	Midlands Postal Region	NI	Northern Ireland Postal Region
NE	North Eastern Postal Region	P	National Postal Museum, divided into:-
NW	North Western Postal Region	PM	Museum and Historic Series cards
SE	South Eastern Postal Region	PC	Publicity cards
		PE	Exhibition an Special Series cards

Cards issued by Head Postmasters, often without the authority of the Regional Board, are shown as '(local)'. Promotional, Postcode and Souvenir cards appear at the end of each regional listing, where issued. These categories of cards issued by Postal Headquarters appear in Section VII.

Some regional cards exist with reverse variations of typesetting, the more interesting being mentioned. Trial printings are also noted where these have been placed on sale. There are other variations not listed such as shade differences, guillotining from both front and back, plate varieties, etc., which make worthwhile additions to a collection.

ERRORS

Errors occur more frequently on Regional cards than on PHQ 'stamp' cards and although not listed they are much sought after. As a guide prices would be:-

Missing colour: £5-£25	Effective shift in colour: £2.50-£7.50
Blank reverse: £7.50-£20	Glazed reverse, unglazed front: £3-£10

CANCELLED CARDS

Where cards exist cancelled on first day of sale the value is shown under FDI followed by a code letter which refers to the type of known relevant cancel as follows:-
- (S) **Special handstamp**
- (F) **FIRST DAY OF ISSUE** town handstamp
- (C) **Circular date stamp** or machine cancel (with or without slogan)

Examples —

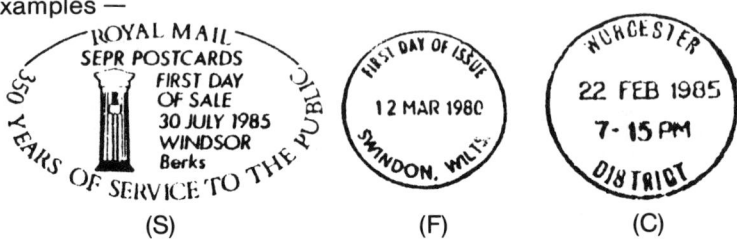

(S)   (F)   (C)

Where a — occurs in the FDI column it means that no first day cancelled cards are known even if a date of issue has been recorded.

Relevant local operational cancels (C) generally command a premium over (S) cancels. Not all the known cancels are listed and in some cases two or more special handstamps (S) exist for the date of issue. Many cards are known cancelled obverse (postage stamp on picture side) but are not listed separately as in the main values are the same as cancelled reverse. From 1 October 1984, when PO regulations were changed, any card may be cancelled obverse with a philatelic handstamp applied to any postage stamp. Prior to that date obverse use was confined to day of issue of appropriate stamp although exceptional uses are known.

POSTAL HEADQUARTERS PROMOTIONAL, COMMEMORATIVE AND SOUVENIR CARDS

The Post Office has issued postcards as souvenirs of special events and for promotional purposes throughout the years since 1890 when Postal Headquarters issued its first card for the Penny Postage Jubilee exhibition at the Guildhall, London in May of that year. The section includes NPM Stamp Bug card, the 1981 national series sold throughout the UK and others sold at selective post offices but also available at the NPM and the Philatelic Bureau, Edinburgh. The cancels known are coded after the value as under 'Cancelled Cards' in the notes on Regional Cards.

POST OFFICE COMMEMORATIVE COVERS

All known official Post Office illustrated covers issued for special events or as souvenir/commemorative items are listed including those jointly sponsored with another organisation where they have only been sold over post office counters. Covers published by commercial organisations or charities which have also been sold at post office counters are not listed. The issuing authority is shown after the catalogue number in abbreviated form, e.g. PHQ for Postal Headquarters, NWPR for North Western Postal Region and similar abbreviations for the other regions. The cancels known are coded after the value as under 'Cancelled Cards' in the notes on Regional Cards. The illustrated 'souvenir' covers issued to visitors on specially arranged tours of PO sorting offices and MLOs, of which many designs are known, have been excluded from the listings.

SECTION VI   REGIONAL CARDS
EASTERN POSTAL REGION

Cards can be obtained from:

Philatelic Counter
9-11 St. Andrews Street
CAMBRIDGE CB1 1AA

Philatelic Counter
29-39 Head Street
COLCHESTER CO1 1AA

Philatelic Counter
City Centre Post Office
MILTON KEYNES MK9 3AA

Easton Postal Board (to 30 Sept. '86)
Charles House, 24, St. Peters Street,
COLCHESTER CO1 1EP

Philatelic Counter
13-17 Bank Plain
NORWICH NR2 4AA

Philatelic Counter
102-4 St. Aldates
OXFORD OX1 1AA

Philatelic Counter
Weston Road
SOUTHEND ON SEA SS1 1AA

		FDI	Mint	
1973, SPRING E1	**OXFORD HEAD POST OFFICE PHILATELIC COUNTER (1-00-01-82E)** Five views, four of Oxford and one of the Philatelic Counter Print 20,000	—	0.35	☐
	Three reverse typesettings known — 1. Code No. 18½mm long. 'I' in 'PHILATELIC' under 'A' in 'OBTAINABLE' 2. Code No. 18½mm long. 'C' in 'PHILATELIC' under 'B' in 'OBTAINABLE' 3. Code No. 19mm long. 'C' under 'B' as 2. - 90p			
1979, 3 OCTOBER E2	**NORWICH PHILATELIC CENTRE (CKPO1)** Five views, four of Norwich and one of the Philatelic Counter Print 24,000 Norwich CDS	1.00(S) 2.00(C)	0.30	☐ ☐ ☐
1980, 25 MARCH E3	**DISS-GISLINGHAM POSTBUS (CKPO2)** Five views on the route of the postbus Print 18,000 Diss, Eye, Occold, Gislingham, Bedingfield CDS	1.00(S) 2.75(C)	0.40	☐ ☐ ☐
1980, 30 JUNE E4	**COLCHESTER POSTBUS (CKCPO1)** Outside Norman Castle at Colchester Print 18,000 Colchester, Ardleigh, Lawford, Stratford St. Mary, Little Bromley, Dedham, East Bergholt CDS	1.00(S) 1.50(C) to £2.75(C)	0.40	☐ ☐ ☐
1980, 13 AUGUST E5	**CAMBRIDGE PHILATELIC CENTRE (CKCM1)** Five views, four of Cambridge and one of the Philatelic Counter Print 24,000 Cambridge CDS	1.00(S) 2.00(C)	0.30	☐ ☐ ☐
N.B.	This card was intended for earlier issue but those printed had two of reverse captions transposed 'The Bridge of Sighs' printed against 'Top right' instead of 'Bottom left' and most were destroyed. (Approximately 30 cards escaped destruction. Price £45).			
1981, 22 JULY E6	**IPSWICH HEAD POST OFFICE (R78693)** Shows the Head Post Office, Cornhill, Ipswich after its opening on 27.7.1881. Print 27,000 Ipswich 'FDI', Ipswich CDS Two reverse typesettings known— 1. Stamp box frame complete 2. Stamp box left frame line broken.	1.00(S) from 1.40(C)	0.25	☐ ☐ ☐
	PICTURESQUE POST OFFICES IN OXFORDSHIRE Set of four in red card folder with photo. of horse drawn mail van outside Oxford HPO.			
1984, 15 FEBRUARY E7	**GREAT TEW, OXFORDSHIRE (CKPO6)** Print 24,300 Oxford, Great Tew/Oxford CDS	1.00(S) from 1.30(C)	0.25	☐ ☐ ☐
1984, 15 FEBRUARY E8	**DORCHESTER-ON-THAMES, OXFORDSHIRE (CKPO7)** Print 24,300 Oxford, Dorchester-on-Thames/Oxford CDS	1.00(S) from 1.30(C)	0.25	☐ ☐ ☐
1984, 15 FEBRUARY E9	**WYTHAM, OXFORDSHIRE (CKPO8)** Print 24,300 Oxford, Wytham/Oxford CDS	1.00(S) from 1.30(C)	0.25	☐ ☐ ☐

		FDI	Mint
1984, 15 FEBRUARY E10	**SWALCLIFFE, OXFORDSHIRE (CKPO9)** Print 24,300 .... Oxford, Banbury/Oxon., Swalcliffe CDS	1.00(S) from 1.30(C)	0.25 ☐ ☐ ☐
E7 - E10	Set of 4 as above with folder	4.00(S)	1.00 ☐ ☐
1985, 8 OCTOBER E11	**OPENING OF LUTON ARNDALE CENTRE POST OFFICE (CKPO10)** Facade of new PO and photos. of Luton Hoo and Town Hall/War Memorial Print 12,000 .... Luton, Beds. CDS or 'FDI'	1.00(S) 1.50(C)(F)	0.25 ☐ ☐ ☐

E1

E2

E4

E8

LT33

LT45

LT17

LT49

LT42

L2

L5

L9

 # COVER ALBUMS

With cover collecting growing in popularity all the time we are proud to offer a comprehensive range of albums to meet the needs of first day cover collector and postal historian alike. All leaves have black card inserts to set off your covers to best advanatage.

1. THE NEW PIONEER COVER ALBUM
A fully padded PVC binder in a choice of black, green or red. Holds up to 50 covers in a high capacity, low priced album, ideal for the beginner.

2. THE PROTECTOR COVER ALBUM
The luxury padded binder comes in deep blue, brown or maroon with gold blocking on the spine and a secure 4-ring arch mechanism. The album contains 15 double and 5 single-pocket leaves, the former being specifically designed to house the current standard British Post Office first day covers. The leaves are made from 'Polyprotec' a material which does not crease or tear easily, and will not degrade and offers considerable protection against heat and ultra violet light. Holds up to 70 covers.

3. THE MALVERN COVER ALBUM
Another great value album suitable for collectors at all levels. The 4-ring arch fitting binder contains 15 double-pocket leaves, 5 single-pocket leaves and holds up to 70 covers in all. Available in blue, green or red.

4. THE NEW CLASSIC COVER ALBUM
A compact de-luxe album with 20 'Polyprotec' leaves offering full protection for up to 40 covers and two clear fly leaves to hold an index of notes. Available in black, red or blue and supplied in a protective slip box.

5. THE SG MAJOR COVER ALBUM
(Not illustrated)
A luxury album recommended for that really special collection. The fully padded, leather grained PVC binder has peg fittings and comes with 15 crystal clear leaves (12 double-pocket and 3 single pocket) and two clear fly leaves in which to insert notes. Available in dark red, deep blue or brown – the top of the range.

6. THE UNIVERSAL COVER ALBUM
The cover album which allows stamps, booklets and presentation packs to be housed all together – please write for details.

and COLLECTA COVERS ALBUMS TOO!
The very popular range of Collecta albums are also available direct from us including the silver Arrow, the Golden Arrow, the M55 and the Supreme – please send for details.

**Stanley Gibbons Publications Ltd
Parkside, Christchurch Road
Ringwood, Hampshire BH24 3SH
Telephone: 042 54 2363**

LONDON POSTAL REGION

Cards can be obtained from:

Philatelic Counter
London Chief Office
King Edward Building
King Edward Street
LONDON EC1A 1AA

Philatelic Counter
Trafalgar Square
24/28 William IV Street
LONDON WC2N 4DL

Philatelic Counter
10 High Street
CROYDON
Surrey CR9 1HT

London Postal Board (to 30 Sept. '86)
148/166 Old Street
LONDON EC1V 9HQ

Philatelic Counter
64 South Street
ROMFORD
Essex RM1 1RL

Post Office Tower Cards
Issued by Post Office Telecommunications under the authority of the Postmaster General. The telecommunications division became 'British Telecom' on separation 1 Oct. 1981.

1966, May — Mint
- LT 1 Tower from Catesby Building (Tel/71) ..... 5.50 ☐
- LT 9 Tower from Mullard Building (Tel/79) ..... 5.50 ☐
- LT10 Tower from Mullard Building (Tel/79) Giant ..... 5.50 ☐
- LT11 Tower from Catesby Building (Tel/84C) ..... 5.50 ☐
- LT12 Tower from Clipstone Building (Tel/83) ..... 5.50 ☐
- LT13 Tower from Torrington Place (GP/51) ..... 5.50 ☐
- LT14 Night view from Tower (GP/52) ..... 3.50 ☐
- LT15 View from Tower looking south-east (T590) Giant ..... 5.50 ☐
- LT16 Tower from Clipstone Street (T618) ..... 5.50 ☐
- LT17 Tower from Charlotte Street (T619) ..... 3.50 ☐
- LT18 Tower from Charlotte Street (T619C) ..... 5.50 ☐
- LT19 Tower from Fitzroy Square (T621) ..... 5.50 ☐
- LT20 Tower from W.D.O. (T623C) ..... 5.50 ☐
- LT21 Tower from W.D.O. (T623C) Giant ..... 5.50 ☐
- LT22 Tower from Mullard Building (T626C) ..... 5.50 ☐
- others probably exist

1967/1968
- LT23 Tower from Fitzroy Square (L1) 20,000 ..... 5.50 ☐
- LT24 Tower from W.D.O. (L7) 20,000 ..... 5.50 ☐
- LT25 Tower from Fitzroy Square (L9) 20,000 ..... 5.50 ☐
- LT26 Tower from Mullard Building (L10) 20,000 ..... 5.50 ☐
- LT27 Night view of Tower (L13) 20,000 ..... 5.50 ☐
- LT28 Tower from Clipstone Street (L14) 20,000 ..... 5.50 ☐
- LT29 Tower from W.D.O. (L7GL) Giant 10,000 ..... 5.00 ☐
- LT30 Tower from Clipstone Street (L14GL) Giant 10,000 ..... 5.00 ☐
- LT31 Night view looking south-east (L15GL) Giant 10,000 ..... 4.50 ☐

1968/1969
- LT32 British Museum and the City (H1) 16,500 ..... 2.25 ☐
- LT33 View of Centre Point (H2) 16,500 ..... 2.25 ☐
- LT34 Westminster from Tower (H3) 16,500 ..... 2.25 ☐

Mint
- LT35 Regents Park from Tower (H4) 16,500 ..... 2.25 ☐
- LT36 Regents park from Tower (H5) 16,500 ..... 5.50 ☐
- LT37 King's Cross from Tower (H6) 16,500 ..... 5.50 ☐

1969
- LT38 Tower from W.D.O. (NL7) 33,000 ..... 1.00 ☐
- LT39 Tower from Mullard Building (NL10) 63,000 ..... 1.00 ☐
- LT40 Night view of Tower (NL13) 86,000 ..... 1.00 ☐
- LT41 Tower from Clipstone Street (NL14) 63,000 ..... 1.00 ☐
- LT42 Tower from Charlotte Place (NL16) 56,000 ..... 1.00 ☐
- LT43 Tower from W.D.O. (NL17) 26,000 ..... 5.00 ☐
- LT44 Tower from W.D.O. (NL7GL) Giant 13,000 ..... 5.50 ☐

1970/1971
- LT45 Night scene from Portland Place (NL20) Imprint 'POST OFFICE' 30,000 ..... 1.00 ☐
- LT46 Charity pool in Tower (NL21) Imprint 'POST OFFICE' 20,000 ..... 1.00 ☐
- LT47 Tower at night (NL22) Imprint 'POST OFFICE' 20,000 ..... 1.00 ☐
- LT48 Tower lit at night (NL23) Imprint 'POST OFFICE' 20,000 ..... 1.00 ☐
- LT49 Tower from Clipstone Street (NL14GL) Giant. Imprint 'GPO' ..... 4.00 ☐
- LT50 Night scene from Portand Place (NL20GL) Giant. Imprint 'POST OFFICE' 60,000 ..... 1.25 ☐
- LT51 Tower from Fitzroy Square (NL24GL) Giant. Imprint 'POST OFFICE' 60,000 ..... 1.25 ☐
- LT52 Three dimensional view from Charlotte Place. Imprint 'POST OFFICE' ..... 1.50 ☐
- LT53 Tower from Clipstone Street (NL14GL) Giant. As LT49 but Imprint 'POST OFFICE' 71,000 ..... 1.25 ☐

There are no F.D.I. with these issues. All may be found used between 19 May '66 and 31 Oct '71 with London W1 m/c with slogan 'Posted at the Post Office Tower' (in transposed position from 6 May '68) from £2.75.

London Postal Region Cards

		FDI	Mint	
1982, 19 JULY	**VIEWS FROM POST OFFICES IN WEST LONDON** (Local)			
L1	Three views—Print 5,000	—	0.50	☐
1982, 6 SEPTEMBER	**A ROYAL MAIL PHILATELIC POSTCARD** (Local)			
L2	Four railway views Print 5,000	—	0.50	☐
1982, 11 OCTOBER	**K-TYPE PILLAR BOX BEHIND THE ROYAL ALBERT HALL (LPR1)**			
L3	Print 20,000	1.00(S)	0.30	☐ ☐
	London SW1/4 CDS or other CDS	1.75(C)		☐
1982, 25 OCTOBER	**A COLLECTION OF CROYDON POSTMARKS (LPR2)**			
L4 (1) 1982, 25 Oct.	Print 15,000	1.00(S)	0.30	☐ ☐
	Croydon/Surrey m/c slogan or London m/c	1.75(C)		☐
(2) 1983, 21 Jun	Overprinted on reverse in grey blue — 'CHARTER CENTENARY CROYDON 1883-1983'	1.75(S)	0.75	☐ ☐
	Croydon/Surrey m/c or CDS	2.00(C)		☐

		FDI	Mint	
1983, 25 APRIL L5	**POST OFFICE UNDERGROUND RAILWAY** Mount Pleasant Station **(LPR3)** Print 20,000 .... London IS MLO, Paddington or other CDS	2.00(S) 2.25(C)	0.45	☐ ☐ ☐
1983, 1 AUGUST L6	**PARCELS CENTENARY (LPR4)** Etching showing an 1883 parcels office and inset — modern sorting office control equipment Print 20,000 .... Hampstead BO CDS or Hampstead SDO CDS	1.00(S) 1.50(C)	0.30	☐ ☐ ☐
	MAIL COACHING INNS. Set of four. Early prints issued to commemorate the 200th anniversary of the first mailcoach.			
1984, 24 JULY L7	**THE STAR AND GARTER AT KEW (LPR5a)** Print 14,000 .... Kew Gardens/Richmond, Surrey CDS	1.00(S) 2.00(C)	0.25	☐ ☐ ☐
1984, 24 JULY L8	**THE GEORGE AT SOUTHWARK (LPR5b)** Print 14,000	1.00(S)	0.25	☐ ☐
1984, 24 JULY L9	**THE COACH AND HORSES AT ILFORD (LPR5c)** Print 14,000 .... Ilford/Romford CDS	1.00(S) 2.00(C)	0.25	☐ ☐ ☐
1984, 24 JULY L10	**THE OLD WHITE LION AT NORTH FINCHLEY (LPR5d)** Print 14,000	1.00(S)	0.25	☐ ☐
L7-10	Set of 4 as above	4.00(S)	1.00	☐ ☐
	350 YEARS OF LONDON POST. Set of four. Issued to celebrate 350th anniversary of Royal Mail.			
1985, 30 JULY L11	**NEWS SHEET OF 1646 (LPR6a)** Print 10,000	1.00(S)	0.25	☐ ☐
1985, 30 JULY L12	**RAILWAY SORTING CARRIAGE 1838 (LPR6b)** Print 10,000	1.00(S)	0.25	☐ ☐
1985, 30 JULY L13	**LOADING MAIL AT CROYDON AIRPORT EARLY 1930s (LPR6c)** Print 10,000	1.00(S)	0.25	☐ ☐
1985, 30 JULY L14	**INTERNATIONAL DATAPOST FROM CITY HELIPORT TO LONDON HEATHROW 1985 (LPR6d)** Print 10,000	1.00(S)	0.25	☐ ☐
L11-14	Set of 4 as above	4.00(S)	1.00	☐ ☐

GB NEW ISSUES

★ **PHQ & REGIONAL CARDS**
★ **WORLDS LARGEST STOCKS OF REGIONAL CARDS**
★ **SPECIAL POSTMARKS**
★ **LOCAL POSTMARKS**
★ **ALL REGIONS – INC. NPM & TELECOM**
★ **FREE LISTS**
★ **NEWSLETTER £1.50 PER ANNUM**

ERIC WILDING
80 KINGSLEY ROAD, NORTHAMPTON, NORTHANTS, NN2 7BL, ENGLAND
Phone: 0604 711538

MIDLANDS POSTAL REGION

Cards can be obtained from:

Philatelic Counter	Philatelic Counter	Philatelic Counter	Philatelic Counter
Victoria Square	163 Corporation Street	4 Bishop Street	St. Giles Street
BIRMINGHAM B1 1BA	COVENTRY CV1 1AB	LEICESTER LE1 1AA	NORTHAMPTON NN1 1AD
Philatelic Counter	Philatelic Counter	Philatelic Counter	Midland Postal Board (to 30 Sept. '86)
Queen Street	25-31 Tontine Street	8-10 Foregate Street	86 Lionel Street
NOTTINGHAM NG1 2BN	Hanley	WORCESTER WR1 1AA	BIRMINGHAM B3 1HQ
	Stoke-on-Trent ST1 1AA		

			FDI	Mint		
1974, 30 OCTOBER	**CHETWYND HOUSE, STAFFORD (MPB CARD 1)**					
M1 (1) 1974, 30 Oct.	1st Print 5,000 (MPB Card 1)		16.00(S)	2.00	☐	☐
(2) 1978, 15 July	2nd print 2,500 (MPB Card 1 (Revised), cream card)		—	1.25		☐
(3) 1978, Oct.	3rd print 3,000 (MPB Card 1 (Revised), white card)		—	0.75		☐
(4) 1979, 3 Sept.	4th print 3,000 (MPB Card 1 Reprint 7/79)		2.00(C)	0.60	☐	☐
(5) 1980, Jan	5th Print 5,200 (MPB Card 1 (1/80))		—	0.25		☐
1974, 30 OCTOBER	**RICHARD BRINSLEY SHERIDAN (MPB CARD 2)**					
M2 (1) 1974, 30 Oct.	1st Print 5,000 (MPB Card 2)		16.00(S)	2.00	☐	☐
(2) 1978, 15 July	2nd Print 2,500 (MPB Card 2 (Revised), cream card)		—	1.25		☐
(3) 1978, Oct.	3rd print 5,000 (MPB Card 2 (Revised), white card)		—	0.75		☐
(4) 1979, 3 Sept.	4th print 3,000 (MPB Card 2 Reprint 7/79)		2.00(C)	0.60	☐	☐
(5) 1980, Jan	5th Print 5,200 (MPB Card 2 (1/80))		—	0.30		☐
1974, 3 DECEMBER	**SIR ROWLAND HILL KCB (MPB CARD 3)**					
M3	Kidderminster					
(1) 1974, 3 Dec.	1st Print 5,000 (MPB Card 3)		15.00(S)	20.00	☐	☐
(2) 1977, Nov.	2nd Print 2,000 (MPB Card 3 (Reprint))		—	2.00		☐
(3) 1978 15 July	3rd Print 5,000 (MPB Card 3 (Revised), cream card)		—	1.75		☐
(4) 1978, Oct.	4th Print 5,000 (MPB Card 3 (Revised), white card, dark brown printing on reverse)		—	1.30		☐
(5) 1979, Jan.	5th Print 5,000 (MPB Card 3 (Revised)), white card, red/brown printing on reverse		—	1.00		☐
(6) 1979, April	6th Print 5,000 (MPB Card 3 (4/79))		—	0.75		☐
(7) 1979, 22 Aug.	7th Print 10,000 (MPB Card 3 (Reprint 7/79))		1.60(S)	0.50	☐	☐
	Various commemorative postmarks		1.75(S)			☐
(8) 1980 Jan.	8th Print 5,200 (MPB Card 3 (1/80))		—	0.30		☐
(9) 1985, 18 April	9th Print 10,000 (MPB Card 3 (Reissued 3/85))		2.00(S)	0.30	☐	☐
1979, 22 AUGUST	**SIR ROWLAND HILL PORTRAIT (MPB CARD 4)**					
M4	Print 6,000 approx.		2.50(S)	1.00	☐	☐

N.B. This card went on sale during Sir Rowland Hill Centenary year and was withdrawn 31 December 1979

A lithographic print of the portrait was issued by MPB in a limited edition of 500.

	VICTORIA SQUARE POST OFFICE, BIRMINGHAM					
	Four cards with information card in pastic pack					
1981, 18 MARCH	**NEW STREET — SITE FOR VICTORIA SQUARE POST OFFICE (MPB Card 9.1)**					
M5	Corbetts Hotel c. 1875 Print 10,000		1.00(S)	0.50	☐	☐
	Birmingham/83 CDS		1.50(C)			☐
1981, 18 MARCH	**VICTORIA SQUARE POST OFFICE, BIRMINGHAM (MPB CARD 9.2)**					
M6	c. 1895 Print 10,000		1.00(S)	0.50	☐	☐
	Birmingham/83 CDS		1.50(C)			☐
1981, 18 MARCH	**VICTORIA SQUARE POST OFFICE, BIRMINGHAM (MPB CARD 9.3)**					
M7	1955 Print 10,000		1.00(S)	0.50	☐	☐
	Birmingham/83 CDS		1.50(C)			☐
1981, 18 MARCH	**VICTORIA SQUARE POST OFFICE, BIRMINGHAM (MPB Card 9.4)**					
M8	1980 Print 10,000		1.00(S)	0.50	☐	☐
	Birmingham/83 CDS		1.50(C)			☐
M5 - 8	Set of 4 as above with information card in pack		4.00(S)	1.80	☐	☐
1981, 31 MARCH	**CENTRE CYCLE OF 1881 AT GLADSTONE POTTERY MUSEUM, LONGTON, STOKE-ON-TRENT**					
M9	In yard with bottle kilns **(MPB 10)**					
(1) 1981, 31 March	Print 15,000 (10,000 and extra 5,000 printed)		1.25(S)	0.35	☐	☐
	Stoke-on-Trent, Longton or Longton B.O. CDS		1.80-4.50(C)			☐
(2) 1986, 9 June	Different reverse print inscribed 'A re-issue of Card MPB10 especially for the National Garden Festival 1986 at Stoke-on-Trent' **(MBP 10R)**					
	Print 10,000		2.00(S)	0.25	☐	☐

			FDI	Mint
1981, 16 JUNE	**MIDLANDS LETTER BOXES — WARWICK AND MALVERN FLUTED**			
M10	2 Doric Column Pillar Boxes **(MPB Card 6)** Print 10,000		1.25(S)	0.50 ☐ ☐
	Warwick & Leamington Spa CDS; Malvern m/c		1.80(C)	☐
1981, 26 JUNE	**ROUS LENCH & RADFORD LETTER BOXES (MPB CARD 5)**			
M11	Print 10,000		1.25(S)	0.50 ☐ ☐
	Rous Lench/Evesham CDS; Worcester CDS	From 1.80(C)		☐
1981, 15 JULY	**DERBY RAM** Mythical beast of Derbyshire **(MPB11)**			
M12	Print 10,000		1.25(S)	0.40 ☐ ☐
	Derby; Alfreton/Derby or Ripley/Derby CDS	1.50-1.80(C)		☐
1981, 8 SEPTEMBER	**HEXAGONAL PENFOLD LETTER BOX, BUDBY, NEWARK (MPB CARD 7)**			
M13	Print 10,000		1.25(S)	0.40 ☐ ☐
	Newark/Notts; Edwinstowe/Mansfield, Notts. or Ollerton/Newark, Notts. CDS	1.50-2.25(C)		☐
1981, 1 OCTOBER	**STOKE ON TRENT HEAD POST OFFICE — 75th ANNIVERSARY OF ITS OPENING (MPB CARD 12)**			
M14	Print 20,000		1.00(S)	0.30 ☐ ☐
	Stoke-on-Trent/Staffs CDS		1.80(C)	☐
1981, 1 DECEMBER	**STANDARD AND K-TYPE POST BOXES (MPB CARD 8)**			
M15	Print 10,000		1.00(S)	0.40 ☐ ☐
	Birmingham/83 CDS		1.50(C)	☐
1982, 1 MARCH	**VICTORIAN STAMP VENDING MACHINE (MPB CARD 13)**			
M16	Print 20,000		1.00(S)	0.30 ☐ ☐
	Birmingham/129 CDS		1.50(C)	☐
	18 SEP '82 Glossop/Derbyshire CDS + cachet 'GLOSSOP VICTORIAN WEEKEND/Sold at Victoria Street Post Office'		8.50(C)	☐

Approx. 300 were cacheted and sold over P.O. counter at Glossop (in NWPR). A posting box was provided for cards to receive 'local' CDS.

	THE NANTWICH MURAL Set of three reproducing the Post Office mural in three sections. Designed by Gerald Rickards.			
1983, 5 JULY	**MURAL — THE LEFT HAND SECTION.** Centre panel with Post Office logo. **(MPB CARD 14.1)**			
M17	Print 10,000		1.00(S)	0.30 ☐ ☐
1983, 5 JULY	**MURAL — CENTRE SECTION.** Parts of Grammar School and St. Mary's Church **(MPB CARD 14.2)**			
M18	Print 10,000		1.00(S)	0.30 ☐ ☐
1983, 5 JULY	**MURAL — RIGHT HAND SECTION.** Representation of Elizabeth I, P.O. Royal Cypher EIIR letter boxes, Nantwich date stamp. **(MPB CARD 14.3)**			
M19	Print 10,000		1.00(S)	0.30 ☐ ☐
M17-19	Set of 3		3.00(S)	0.90 ☐ ☐
	Nantwich/Cheshire CDS or m/c		3.25(C)	☐

Booklet 'Nantwich Town Trail' based on the mural with set of cards in fold of booklet £1.30.

1985, 22 JANUARY	**'ROWLAND HILL' LOCO. 1885 (MPB CARD 15)** An artists impression of the engine			
M20	Print 15,000		1.00(S)	0.30 ☐ ☐
	Crewe 'FDI' CDS; 'Cheshire' CDS or m/c; Crewe-Cardiff or other TPO CDS on Train commem.	1.40-2.00(C)		☐
1985, 22 FEBRUARY	**WORCESTER PHILATELIC COUNTER MURAL (MPB 16)** Depicts a 'Patent Mail Coach' Artist – Tony Blakemore			
M21	Print 10,000		1.00(S)	0.30 ☐ ☐
	Worcester/District CDS or Phil. Counter handstamp		1.50(C)(S)	☐

N.B. To mark 350 years of Post Office service three breweries issued sets of cards featuring old coaching inns in the Midlands which were sold at the inns and at three Philatelic Counters from 30 July 1985.

			FDI	Mint
	Ansells Brewery issued 6 cards — sold at Birmingham Counter. Manns Brewery issued 6 cards — sold at Northampton Counter. Home Brewery issued 5 cards — sold at Nottingham Counter.			
	Four celebration mail coach runs were arranged by the Post Office 29-31 July. Post Office cachets were applied to items carried on the coach at Grantham & Nottingham on 31 July.			
1985, 31 JULY M22	**WORCESTERSHIRE POSTMARKS 1720-1840 (MPB 17)** Print 10,000 Worcester CDS		1.00(S) 1.50(C)	0.25 ☐ ☐ ☐
N.B.	Worcestershire postmarks 1844-1985 card expected late 1985 was not issued.			
1986, 27 SEPTEMBER M23	**RESTORED 1930's MOBILE POST OFFICE, GPO2 (MPB18)** Vehicle rebuilt at P.O. workshops at Corby Print 10,000 Corby CDS		1.00(S) 1.50(C)	0.25 ☐ ☐ ☐
1986, 27 SEPTEMBER M24	**MORRIS MINOR 1000 POST VAN (MPB19)** Original condition, from Museum of British Road Transport, Coventry Print 10,000 Coventry CDS or Philatelic Counter handstamp		1.00(S) 1.50(C)(S)	0.25 ☐ ☐ ☐

PROMOTIONAL AND POSTCODE CARDS

1976, — NOVEMBER MP1	**'DERBY RAM' POSTCODE NOTIFICATION — DE5** Official Paid card. Reverse text 'We trust that you will amend your records accordingly' **(MPB/CNP/180)** Print 36,500		—	2.50 ☐
1976, — NOVEMBER MP2	**'DERBY RAM' POSTCODE NOTIFICATION — DE55** Official Paid card. Reverse text 'Can you please use it when you write to me in future?' **(MPB/CNP/180)** Print 43,500		—	2.75 ☐
1982, — JUNE MP3	**CREWE 'USE THE POSTCODE'** Illus. by Nantwich artist J. Haydn Jones Print 10,000		—	1.00 ☐

BRITISH PO REGIONAL AND NATIONAL POSTCARDS SOUVENIR AND PO VISIT COVERS

are our specialty. Send SAE for latest list.

POSTAL BID SALES

held at regular intervals. Unused cards, FD used including CDS, varieties, etc; FD covers and Postal History/Postal Mechanisation items. Send large SAE for illustrated catalogue.

REJUN COVERCARDS

P.O. BOX 8, MARPLE, STOCKPORT SK6 5PY
Tel. 061-427 3275

NORTH EASTERN POSTAL REGION

Cards can be obtained from:

Philatelic Counter Forster House BRADFORD BD1 4TW	**Philatelic Counter** Crown Street DARLINGTON DL1 1AB	**Philatelic Counter** 33 Silver Street DURHAM DH1 3RE	**Philatelic Counter** 64 Victoria Street GRIMSBY DN31 1AA
Philatelic Counter Cambridge Road HARROGATE HG1 1AA	**Philatelic Counter** Jameson Street HULL HU1 3JG	**Philatelic Counter** City Square LEEDS LS1 2UH	**Philatelic Counter** 19-20 Guildhall Street LINCOLN LN1 1AA
Philatelic Counter 59-61 Grange Road MIDDLESBROUGH TS1 5HT	**Philatelic Counter** St. Nicholas Street NEWCASTLE-UPON-TYNE NE1 1AA	**Philatelic Counter** Fitzalan Square SHEFFIELD S1 1AA	**Philatelic Counter** 43-45 Market Square SUNDERLAND SR1 3LL
Philatelic Counter 22 Lendal YORK YO1 2DA	**North Eastern Postal Board** (to 30 Sept. '86) Royal Mail House 29 Wellington Street LEEDS LS1 1DA		

			FDI	Mint		
	YORKSHIRE DALES — First series. Five cards of reproductions of paintings by E. Charlton Taylor, Sub Postmaster of Summerbridge (since retired).					
1974, 4 APRIL NE1	**TAN HILL (NEPR1)** Print 30,000		12.00(S)	0.50	☐	☐
1974, 4 APRIL NE2	**SWINSTY NORWOOD EDGE (NEPR2)** Print 30,000		12.00(S)	0.50	☐	☐
1974, 4 APRIL NE3	**HIGHER REACHES OF WHARFE AT DEEPDALE (NEPR3)** Print 30,000		12.00(S)	0.50	☐	☐
1974, 4 APRIL NE4	**KILNSEY, WHARFEDALE (NEPR4)** Print 30,000		12.00(S)	0.50	☐	☐
1974, 4 APRIL NE5	**MALHAM IN AIREDALE (NEPR5)** Print 30,000		12.00(S)	0.50	☐	☐
NE1 - 5	Set of 5 originally issued in a sealed cellophane pack		60.00(S)	2.50	☐	☐
N.B.	The first printing was 20,000 with an extra print of 10,000 indistinguishable from the first print – except 1st print in polythene wrapper — 2nd in cellophane.					
	YORKSHIRE DALES — Second series. Five cards of reproductions of paintings by E. Charlton Taylor.					
1980, 20 AUGUST NE6	**MUKER IN SWALEDALE (NEPR6)** Print 20,000		1.00(S)	0.30	☐	☐
1980, 20 AUGUST NE7	**GOUTHWAITE, UPPER NIDDERDALE (NEPR7)** Print 20,000		1.00(S)	0.30	☐	☐
1980, 20 AUGUST NE8	**CASTLE BOLTON, WENSLEYDALE (NEPR8)** Print 20,000		1.00(S)	0.30	☐	☐
1980, 20 AUGUST NE9	**HUBBERHOLME, UPPER WHARFEDALE (NEPR9)** Print 20,000		1.00(S)	0.30	☐	☐
1980, 20 AUGUST NE10	**APPLETREEWICK, WHARFEDALE (NEPR10)** Print 20,000		1.00(S)	0.30	☐	☐
NE6 - 10	Set of 5 originally issued in a sealed cellophane pack		5.00(S)	1.50	☐	☐
	NORTH EAST BRIDGES. Six cards — views of bridges within the N.E. Postal Region.					
1981, 17 JULY NE11	**THE HUMBER BRIDGE (NEPR11)** Officially opened by the Queen on the issue date Print 20,000 Hessle Hull, Barton-upon-Humber special handstamp... from Hull, Hessle CDS .... from		1.00(S) 1.50(S) 1.80(C)	0.30	☐ ☐ ☐	☐
1981, 17 JULY NE12	**HIGH LEVEL AND SWING BRIDGES (NEPR12)** Newcastle-upon-Tyne Print 20,000 Newcastle-on-Tyne CDS		1.00(S) 2.30(C)	0.30	☐ ☐	☐
1981, 17 JULY NE13	**THE ROYAL BORDER BRIDGE (NEPR13)** Berwick-upon-Tweed Print 20,000 Berwick-on-Tweed m/c slogan		1.00(S) 2.00(C)	0.30	☐ ☐	☐

			FDI	Mint	

1981, 17 JULY
NE14
THE TRANSPORTER BRIDGE (NEPR14)
Middlesbrough
Print 20,000 .... 1.00(S) 0.30 ☐ ☐
Cleveland m/c slogan .... 2.00(C) ☐

1981, 17 JULY
NE15
THE WEARMOUTH BRIDGE (NEPR15)
Sunderland
Print 20,000 .... 1.00(S) 0.30 ☐ ☐
Sunderland CDS... 2.50(C) ☐

1981, 17 JULY
NE16
THE VIADUCT (NEPR16)
Knaresborough
Print 20,000
Leeds; Knaresborough CDS............................ from 1.00(S) 0.30 ☐ ☐
2.00(C) ☐

NE11 - 16   Set of 6 originally issued in a sealed cellophane pack .... 5.00(S) 1.70 ☐ ☐

1984, 16 JULY
NE17
DARLINGTON PHILATELIC COUNTER (local)
B/W enlargement of Darlington Philatelic Counter handstamp
(1) 1984, 16 July   1st Print 450 (size 89mm x 140mm)....................... 3.00(S) 1.50 ☐ ☐
Darlington CDS... 5.00(C)
(2) 1984, 3 August   2nd Print 650 (size 89mm x 138mm) .... 5.00(S) 1.30 ☐ ☐

N.B. 2nd Print back-dated with Darlington 'Official Opening of Counter' 16 July – £1.50(S).

1984, 1 OCTOBER
DARLINGTON PHILATELIC COUNTER (local)
As NE17 with address of B.O. and telephone number on front. Reverse with additional wording '1st October 15th anniversary of Post Office Corporation'.
NE18
Print 1,500 (also known FD obverse) .... 1.30(S) 1.00 ☐ ☐
Darlington CDS, NE TPO CDS .... from 2.25(C) ☐

1984, 20 NOVEMBER
DARLINGTON PHILATELIC COUNTER (local)
As NE17 but small print of address and telephone number front left. Reverse with 'A' Merry Christmas from Darlington Philatelic Counter' at left
NE19
Print 2,500... 1.25(S) 0.40 ☐ ☐
Darlington CDS; Darlington 'FDI' .... 1.50(C)(F) ☐

N.B. A wallet size 1985 calendar card with illustration of Philatelic Counter handstamp was also issued 20 November.

1985, 22 JANUARY
STOCKTON & DARLINGTON RAILWAY "LOCOMOTION" (1825) (local)
Reverse — Enlargement of Darlington Philatelic Counter handstamp in blue
NE20
Print 5,000 **(Serial No. 4)**.................................. 1.25(S) 0.30 ☐ ☐
Darlington CDS, Darlington 'FDI' or TPO CDS........... 1.50(C)(F) ☐

1985, 22 JANUARY
NE21
FAMOUS TRAINS THROUGH YORK (local)
B/W drawing of 'Flying Scotsman'
Print 10,000 .... 1.00(S) 0.30 ☐ ☐
York CDS. York 'FDI'. Phil Ctr. handstamp TPO CDS .... from 1.25(C)(S) ☐

1986, 22 MAY
NE22
YORK HEAD P.O. – PHILATELIC COUNTER (NEPR17)
Five views, four rural post offices; Centre – Philatelic counter at Lendal, York
Print 18,000 .... 1.00(S) 0.25 ☐ ☐
Malton/N. Yks. CDS; a York TPO or other CDS............... 1.50(C) ☐

1986, 22 MAY
NE23
HULL HEAD P.O. — PHILATELIC COUNTER (NEPR18)
Five views, four rural post offices; Centre – Philatelic counter at Jameson Street, Hull
Print 18,000 .... 1.00(S) 0.25 ☐ ☐
Hull CDS or other CDS....................................... 1.50(C) ☐

1986, 22 SEPTEMBER
NE24
SHEFFIELD GENERAL POST OFFICE (local)
Sepia photo of the Victorian building; issued to visitors on open day 21 September. Postings that day received Sheffield Philatelic Counter spec. handstamp 22 SEP '86. Print 1,000
Sheffield Philatelic Counter special handstamp.............. 2.00(S) 0.50 ☐ ☐
1.75(S) ☐

PROMOTIONAL, POSTCODE AND SOUVENIR CARDS

		FDI	Mint	
1974, 15 JUNE NEP1	**SHEFFIELD HEAD POST OFFICE OPEN DAY** Souvenir programme (A folded card) Print 1,000.	5.00(S)	—	☐
1976, 18 SEPTEMBER NEP2	**YORK M.L.O. STAFF INVITATION DAY** Souvenir single sided card Print 1,360. Cancelled 29 Sept. '76 York MLO m/c slogan	33.00(S) 36.00(C)	—	☐ ☐
1977, 2 APRIL NEP3	**DONCASTER (MLO) STAFF OPEN DAY** Souvenir card (double sided) Photos of MLO equipment Print 430.	20.00(S)	—	☐
N.B.	A few are known phos. coded — £25.			
1982, — AUGUST NEP4	**CLEVELAND STAMP BUG** Holding notice 'Come to Cleveland's Philatelic Counter' Print 10,000. Cancelled 4 Jan '83 Cleveland Philatelic Counter handstamp — First day of use.	 23.00(S)	 22.00	 ☐ ☐
1982, — NOVEMBER NEP5	**HARROGATE STAMP BUG** Holding notice 'Come to Harrogate's New Philatelic Counter' Print 50,000. Cancelled 15 Nov '82 Harrogate 'Post Office Philatelic Counter opened'.	 25.00(C)	 3.00	 ☐ ☐
1983, — MAY NEP6	**GRIMSBY STAMP BUG** Holding notice 'Come to Grimsby's New Philatelic Counter'. Drawing of the Humber Bridge as background. Print 55,000. Cancelled 25 May '83 Grimsby 'Post Office Philatelic Counter opened' (also obverse).	 15.00(S)	 6.00	 ☐ ☐
1983 — JUNE NEP7	**'ROYAL MAIL PARCELS' PARADE FLOAT** Lorry with 'parcel' which entered carnival parades in NEPR. Prize draw on reverse			
(1) 1983, — June (2) 1983, — —	1st Print – Guillotined from front. 2nd print — Guillotined from back. Cancelled 3 Aug '83 Leeds CDS Cancelled 26 Oct '83 NPM Maltese Cross handstamp (FD of sale at NPM).	 15.00(C) 25.00(S)	2.50 0.90	☐ ☐ ☐ ☐
N.B.	Known also with reverse printing 'See us at The Lincolnshire Show June 22 and 23' etc. 1st paid imprint – £15.			
1984 — JULY NEP8	**DARLINGTON STAMP BUG** Holding notice 'Come to Darlington's New Philatelic Counter'. Drawing of Clock Tower in background (Featured in Counter handstamp) Print 50,000. Cancelled 16 July '84 Darlington 'Official Opening Philatelic Counter'.	 12.50(S)	 2.75	 ☐ ☐
1984, 1 OCTOBER NEP9	**YORK MAIN POST OFFICE COUNTER — OFFICIAL REOPENING** Souvenir card — also worded 'Centenary of PO Building at 22 Lendal, York YO1 2DA' Reverse blank – issued as a table place card but sold at Philatelic Counter Print 1,000. York CDS; m/c slogan or TPO CDS.	 3.50(S) 4.00(C)	 6.00	 ☐ ☐ ☐
1985, — JUNE NEP10	**WE'RE MOVING . . . STAMP BUG — CLEVELAND** Holding notice 'Come to Cleveland's New Philatelic Counter' and drawing of workmen with large letters MOVING. Reverse publicising new Middlesbrough PO opening 10 June Print 2,000. Cancelled 10 June '85 'To commemorate the opening of the new Middlesbrough Branch PO'.	 20.00(S)	 12.00	 ☐ ☐

NE1

NE2

NE10

NE11

NE12

NE14

NE17

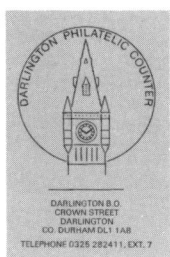
NE18

NE19

NE20

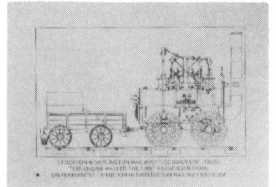
NE21

NE22

NE24

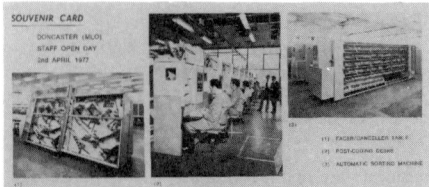
NEP3

NEP10

NORTH WESTERN POSTAL REGION

Cards can be obtained from:

Philatelic Counter	**Philatelic Counter**	**Philatelic Counter**	**Philatelic Counter**
Abingdon Street	124 Deansgate	20-34 Warwick Road	Whitechapel
BLACKPOOL FY1 1AA	BOLTON BL1 1AA	CARLISLE CA1 1AA	LIVERPOOL L1 1AA
Philatelic Counter	**Philatelic Counter**	**North Western Postal Board** (to 30 Sept. '86)	
Spring Gardens	80-83 St. Peter's Precinct	St. James's Building	
MANCHESTER M2 1AA	OLDHAM OL1 1AD	79 Oxford Street	
		MANCHESTER M60 1DA	

		FDI	Mint		
1974, 1 MARCH	**DUDDON VALLEY POSTBUS**				
NW1	One view of the Postbus in Broughton in Furness				
(1) 1974, 1 March	1st Print 2,000 (No code number on reverse, first line of description begins "Lancs"...)	31.00(S)	2.75	☐	☐
(2) 1974, — April	2nd Print 2,000 (Code number LA1 on reverse)	—	1.50		☐
(3) 1978, 25 May	3rd Print 10,000 (No code number of reverse, first line of description begins "A Royal Mail...")	10.00(C)	0.75	☐	☐

N.B. All prints known used with cachet 'POSTED ON THE ROYAL MAIL BUS/DUDDON VALLEY'.

1974, 8 APRIL	**PENRITH-MARTINDALE POSTBUS**				
NW2	One view of the Postbus near Ullswater				
(1) 1974, 8 April	1st Print 1,000 (No code number on reverse)	—	66.00		☐
(2) 1974, — —	2nd Print 1,000 (Code no. CA1 on reverse, last line of description begins "Where"...)	—	2.00		☐
	Two reverse typesettings known —				
	1. Second address line 1mm shorter at left				
	2. Five address lines of equal length — £50				
(3) 1978, 25 May	3rd Print 10,000 (Code no. CA1 on reverse, last line of description begins "There"...)	10.00(C)	0.75	☐	☐

N.B. All prints known used with cachet 'POSTED ON THE ROYAL MAIL BUS/PENRITH TO MARTINDALE'.

1976, 11 NOVEMBER	**LIVERPOOL & MANCHESTER RAILWAY (NWPB Mail Transport 1)**				
NW3	Two trains carrying mail and passengers				
(1) 1976, 11 November	1st Print 6,500 (Pink sky, highly glazed)	11.00(C)	12.00	☐	☐

N.B. A 'Ticket' cachet was available at five original sales points — Liverpool, Manchester, Warrington, Blackpool and Wigan. It was available for later prints at Liverpool and Manchester Philatelic Counters and at NWPB office.

(2) 1976, — November	2nd Print 10,000 (Dirty yellow appearance). Printed mid November and back.dated 11 NOV at Warrington to complete FD orders — £15).	—	1.60		☐
(3) 1978, — March	3rd Print 5,000 (Dirty grey appearance)	—	1.00		☐
(4) 1978, 25 May	4th Print 10,000 (Rough card, blue sky)	—	0.75		☐
(5) 1979, 17 September	5th Print 10,000 (Inscribed 4th Reprint) Liverpool; Manchester CDS	1.25(C)	0.50	☐	☐
(6) 1980, 12 March	6th Print 10,000 (Inscribed 5th Reprint)	1.25(S)	0.50	☐	☐
(7) 1980, 12 March	7th Print 75,000 (Inscribed 6th Reprint and has the 150th anniversary logo on front.) Only available with set of Liverpool and Manchester Railway stamps affixed on the reverse.	2.50(S)	—		☐
(8) 1980, 6 May	8th Print 21,200 (Inscribed 7th Reprint. Intended to be released 7th May but sold at the London 1980 Exhibition on the 6th May.	1.00(S)	0.30	☐	☐
(9) 1980, 20 August	9th Print 19,800 (Inscribed 8th Reprint)	1.50(S)	0.30	☐	☐
	Liverpool; Manchester CDS	1.50(C)			☐

N.B. Official cachets (not Post Office) were in use throughout 1980 at Edge Hill Station, Liverpool and Liverpool Road Station, Manchester.

See NW7 for Liverpool and Manchester Railway card depicting trains carrying goods and cattle.

1979, 4 JUNE	**PENRITH-MARTINDALE POSTBUS**				
NW4	Five views of the Postbus				
(1) 1979, 4 June	1st Print 4,000 (Inscribed 1st Print)	2.50(S)	2.50	☐	☐
(2) 1979, 13 August	2nd Print 2,500 (Inscribed 2nd print)	1.25(C)	1.00	☐	☐
	Released by one HPO late July.				
(3) 1980, 16th August	3rd Print 10,000 (Inscribed 3rd Print)	1.50(S)	0.30	☐	☐
	(See NW2 for one view Penrith Postbus Card).				

		FDI	Mint	

1979, 4 JUNE — **DUDDON VALLEY POSTBUS**
NW5
Five winter views of the Postbus
(1) 1979, 4 June — 1st Print 4,000 (Inscribed 1st Print) .... 2.50(S) 2.50 ☐ ☐
(2) 1979, 13 August — 2nd Print 2,500 (Inscribed 2nd Print) .... 1.25(C) 1.00 ☐ ☐
Released by one HPO late July.
(3) 1980, 16 April — 3rd Print 10,000 (Inscribed 3rd Print) .... 1.50(C) 0.30 ☐ ☐

1979, 4 JUNE — **GRIZEDALE FOREST POSTBUS**
NW6
Five views of the Postbus
(1) 1979, 4 June — 1st Print 7,500 (Inscribed 1st Print) .... 1.50(S) 0.50 ☐ ☐
Special Ulverston postmark and cachet 'Posted on the Royal
Mail Bus Grizedale Forest' .... 1.75(S) ☐
(2) 1979, 13 August — 2nd Print 20,000 (Inscribed 2nd Print) .... 1.25(C) 0.30 ☐ ☐
Released by one HPO late July.

N.B. Two official proof sheets in colour of the Penrith/Martindale, Duddon Valley and Grizedale Forest Postbus Original prints were released by NWPB.

1979, 12 MARCH — **LIVERPOOL AND MANCHESTER RAILWAY (NWPB2)**
NW7
Two trains carrying goods and cattle
(1) 1980, 12 March — 1st print 25,000 (Inscribed 1st Print) .... 1.25(S) 0.60 ☐ ☐
(1L) 1980, 12 March — 1st Print 75,000 (Inscribed 1st Print and has 150th Anniversary logo on front). Only available with set of Liverpool and Manchester Railway stamps affixed to the reverse. Liverpool or Manchester special Engine Wheel cancel .... 2.50(S) — ☐
(2) 1980, 24 May — 2nd Print 19,800 (inscribed 2nd print) .... 1.25(C) 0.30 ☐ ☐
Liverpool/St. Helens special postmarks .... 1.30(S) ☐
Prints (1) and (2) exist with —
1. No comma after 'Carriages'
2. Comma after 'Carriages' in last line of wording on front

See NW3 for Liverpool and Manchester Railway card depicting trains carrying mail and passengers.

VICTORIAN POST BOXES. Set of four Drawings by John R. Slawson. **NWPB Series 3**

1981, 13 MAY — **LIVERPOOL SPECIAL POSTBOX 1863 (NWPB Series 3(a))**
NW8
Shows last remaining box of this type still in use
(1) 1981, 13 May — 1st Print 6,900 (Inscribed FIRST PRINT) .... 1.50(S) 0.60 ☐ ☐
Liverpool/22 CDS .... 1.75(C) ☐
Liverpool 'FDI' on Butterfly Commem. .... 1.75(C) ☐
(2) 1981, 24 June — 2nd Print 10,000 (Inscribed SECOND PRINT) .... 1.00(F) 0.30 ☐ ☐
Liverpool/22 CDS .... 1.50(C) ☐

1981, 13 MAY — **FIRST NATIONAL STANDARD POSTBOX WITH LAMP-POST, ROCHDALE (NWPB Series 3(b))**
NW9
(1) 1981, 13 May — 1st Print 6,900 (Inscribed FIRST PRINT) .... 1.50(S) 0.60 ☐ ☐
Rochdale/Lancs. CDS .... 1.75(C) ☐

N.B. Cachet 'ROCHDALE/TOAD LANE — POSTED IN THE BOX' was available at Rochdale — £2.00.

(2) 1981, 24 June — 2nd Print 10,000 (Inscribed SECOND PRINT) .... 1.00(F) 0.30 ☐ ☐
Rochdale/Lancs. CDS or m/c slogan .... 1.50(C) ☐

1981, 13 MAY — **HEXAGONAL PENFOLD POSTBOX BUXTON c.1879 (NWPB Series 3(c))**
NW10
(1) 1981, 13 May — 1st Print 6,900 (Inscribed FIRST PRINT) .... 1.50(S) 0.60 ☐ ☐
Buxton/Derbyshire CDS .... 1.75(C) ☐
(2) 1981, 24 June — 2nd Print 10,000 (Inscribed SECOND PRINT) .... 1.00(F) 0.30 ☐ ☐
Buxton/Derbyshire CDS .... 1.50(C) ☐

1981, 13 MAY — **ANONYMOUS CYLINDRICAL LOW APERATURE POSTBOX, KESWICK c.1885 (NWPB Series 3(d))**
NW11
(1) 1981, 13 May — 1st Print 6,900 (Inscribed FIRST PRINT) .... 1.50(S) 0.60 ☐ ☐
Keswick/Cumbria CDS .... 1.75(C) ☐
known with a variety of special handstamps .... from 1.50(S) ☐
(2) 1981, 24 June — 2nd Print 10,000 (Inscribed SECOND PRINT) .... 1.00(S) 0.30 ☐ ☐
Keswick/Cumbria CDS .... 1.50(C) ☐
known with a variety of special handstamps .... from 1.50(C) ☐

NW8-11 (1) — 1st Prints. Set of 4 as above .... 5.00(S) 2.40 ☐ ☐
NW8-11 (2) — 2nd Prints. Set of 4 as above .... 4.00(F) 1.20 ☐ ☐

			FDI	Mint	

1981, 1 OCTOBER
NW12
NWPB HOT AIR BALLOON (NWPB Series 6(a))
Print 13,400 .... 1.25(S) 0.45 ☐ ☐
Manchester or Liverpool 'Codesort' special handstamp...... 2.00(S) ☐
Exists 149mm x 103½mm or 149mm x 107mm. This card was issued on Post Office Vesting Day to promote the use of postcodes.

N.B. Cachet 'Flown by Royal Mail Hot Air Balloon' was applied to flown cards — £2.00.

VICTORIAN POST BOXES. Second set of four Drawings by John R. Slawson. **NWPB Series 4**

1981, 7 OCTOBER
NW13
FLUTED POSTBOX BIRKENHEAD (NWPB Series 4(a))
All inscribed FIRST PRINT. No second print was issued.
Print 10,500 .... 1.00(S) 0.30 ☐ ☐
Birkenhead/Merseyside CDS .... 1.50(C) ☐

N.B. Cachet 'Posted in the Box — BIRKENHEAD' was available at Birkenhead — £1.50.

1981, 7 OCTOBER
NW14
NATIONAL STANDARD POSTBOX LIVERPOOL c.1863 (NWPB Series 4 (b))
Print 10,500 .... 1.00(S) 0.30 ☐ ☐
Liverpool CDS and various special handstamps......... from 1.25(C)(S) ☐

1981, 7 OCTOBER
NW15
ANONYMOUS CYLINDRICAL HIGH APERTURE POSTBOX, BOLTON c.1881 (NWPB Series 4(c))
Print 10,500 .... 1.00(S) 0.30 ☐ ☐
Bolton/Bury, Wigan CDS .... 1.50(C) ☐

1981, 7 OCTOBER
NW16
VR PILLAR BOX c.1900 (NWPB Series 4 (d))
Print 10,500 .... 1.00(S) 0.30 ☐ ☐
Manchester CDS and various special handstamps...... from 1.25(C)(S) ☐
NW13-16 Set of 4 as above .... 4.00(S) 1.20 ☐ ☐

POST VICTORIAN PILLAR BOXES. Set of four Drawings by John R. Slawson. **NWPB Series 5.** All inscribed FIRST PRINT. No second print was issued.

1981, 18 NOVEMBER
NW17
DOUBLE APERTURE BOX, PRESTON c. 1935 (NWPB Series 5(a))
Print 13,700 .... 1.00(S) 0.30 ☐ ☐
Preston 'Lancashire FDI' or 'Lancashire' CDS........... from 1.25 (F)(C) ☐

1981, 18 NOVEMBER
NW18
E VIII PILLAR BOX, BLACKPOOL c. 1936 (NWPB Series 5(b))
Print 13,700 .... 1.00(S) 0.30 ☐ ☐
Fylde, Blackpool, Wyre, Lancs. 'FDI' or CDS............. from 1.25 (F)(C) ☐

N.B. Cachet 'Posted in the box — E VIII R' was available at Blackpool — £1.50.

1981, 18 NOVEMBER
NW19
E II R PILLAR BOX 1953-1980 (NWPB Series 5 (c))
Print 13,700 .... 1.00(S) 0.30 ☐ ☐
Oldham 'FDI' or Oldham/Lancs. CDS .... from 1.25(F)(C) ☐

1981, 18 NOVEMBER
NW20
'K' TYPE PILLAR BOX, MANCHESTER 1980 (NWPB Series 5(d))
Print 13,700 .... 1.00(S) 0.30 ☐ ☐
Manchester 'FDI' and various special handstamps ...... from 1.25(F)(S) ☐
NW17-20 Set of 4 as above .... 4.00(S) 1.20 ☐ ☐

POST OFFICE TRANSPORTATION IN NWPR
Set of five. **NWPB Series 7**

1982, 20 JULY
NW21
MAIL BY HOVERCRAFT RHYL TO WALLASEY 20th ANNIVERSARY (NWPB Series 7 (a))
Print 12,000 .... 1.00(S) 0.45 ☐ ☐
Wallasey '20th Anniv. Hovercraft Service' and alternative handstamp. .... 1.25(S) ☐

N.B. Cachet 'CARRIED ON 20th ANNIVERSARY HOVERCRAFT' was available at Liverpool for both Wallasey handstamp — £1.75.

1982, 20 JULY
NW22
POST OFFICE TRAM, BLACKPOOL (NWPB Series 7 (b))
Print 12,000 .... 1.00(S) 0.45 ☐ ☐
Blackpool 'Travelling Tram Post Office' Spec. handstamp .... 1.25(S) ☐

N.B. Cachet 'Posted on the World's First Post Office Tram' was available at Blackpool — £1.50.

		FDI	Mint	
1982, 20 JULY	**MAILS OPERATIONS, SPEKE SPOKE, LIVERPOOL** (NWPB Series 7 (c))			
NW23	Print 12,000	1.00(S)	0.45	☐ ☐
	Liverpool/22 CDS.	1.50(C)		☐
1982, 20 JULY	**NWPB HOT AIR BALLOON (NWPB Series 7 (d))**			
NW24	Print 12,000	1.00(S)	0.45	☐ ☐
	Manchester 'Codesort' Spec. handstamp....................	1.50(C)		☐
N.B.	Cachet 'Flown by Royal Mail Balloon' was applied at Manchester to cards flown (at Glossop) —£2.00.			
1982, 20 JULY	**DELIVERY OF MAIL BY BOAT TO PIEL ISLAND** 'Name printed on card as PEIL'. **(NWPB Series 7 (e))**			
NW25	Print 12,000	1.00(S)	0.45	☐ ☐
	Barrow-in-Furness/Cumbria CDS...........................	1.50(C)		☐
NW21-25	Set of 5 as above	5.00(S)	2.25	☐ ☐
1982, 18 OCTOBER	**NWPB 1983 PHILATELIC CALENDAR** containing tear-out postcards of Series 3, 4 and 5 twelve pillar boxes with 'CALENDAR PRINT' on the reverse of each card...	12.50(S)	4.00	☐ ☐
	Twelve diff. 'local' CDS (or m/c)	15.00(C)		☐
	OUR SERVICE TO YOU. Set of four. Four views each card with relevant P.O. datestamp. **NWPB Series 8**			
1983, 10 OCTOBER	**MECHANISED LETTER OFFICES.** Four stages of letter mechanisation process. **(NWPB Series 8(a))**			
NW26	Print 10,000	1.00(S)	0.35	☐ ☐
	Liverpool; Manchester; Preston 'Lancashire'; Bolton CDS or m/c.. from	1.50(C)		☐
	Liverpool; Manchester 'Codesort' special handstamp........	1.50(C)		☐
1983, 10 OCTOBER	**PHILATELIC COUNTERS.** Locations of four of NWPB's philatelic counters. **(NWPB Series 8(b))**			
NW27	Print 10,000	1.00(S)	0.35	☐ ☐
	Blackpool; Oldham; Liverpool or Manchester Philatelic Counter Special handstamps	1.50(S)		☐
1983, 10 OCTOBER (NWPB Series 8(c))	**SUB POST OFFICES.** Four of NWPB's Sub Post Offices.			
NW28	Print 10,000	1.00(S)	0.35	☐ ☐
	Ambleside; Roby Mill Skelmersdale; Lymm; Burnley CDS.... from	1.50(C)		☐
1983, 10 OCTOBER	**RURAL POSTMEN.** Four of NWPB's Rural Postmen on their daily round. **(NWPB Series 8(d))**			
NW29	Print 10,000	1.00(S)	0.35	☐ ☐
	Burnley m/c; Hyde CDS or m/c; Keswick CDS or m/c; Northwich CDS or m/c.. from	1.50(C)		☐
NW26-29	Set of 4	4.00(S)	1.30	☐ ☐
	THE POST OFFICE AT THE GARDEN FESTIVAL Set of four. Watercolours by K. Mosley. **(NWPB Series 9)**			
1984, 2 MAY	**THE ROSE GARDEN (NWPB Series 9(a))**			
NW30	Print 10,000	1.00(S)	0.35	☐ ☐
	Liverpool/22 CDS or m/c slogan 'IGF – LIVERPOOL 84'.....	1.50(C)		☐
	Liverpool 'Queen opens the Garden Festival' handstamp....	1.25(S)		☐
1984, 2 MAY	**"LIVERPOOL SPECIAL" PILLAR BOX AT HERCULANEUM ENTRANCE (NWPB Series 9(b))**			
NW31	Print 10,000	1.00(S)	0.35	☐ ☐
	Liverpool CDS, m/c and handstamp as NW30.......... from	1.25(C)(S)		☐
1984, 2 MAY	**PILLAR BOX AT FULWOOD ENTRANCE (NWPB Series 9(c))**			
NW32	Print 10,000	1.00(S)	0.35	☐ ☐
	Liverpool CDS, m/c and handstamp as NW30.......... from	1,25(C)(S)		☐
1984, 2 MAY	**THE SMALLEST TRAVELLING POST OFFICE IN THE WORLD (NWPB Series 9(d))**			
NW33	Print 10,000	1.00(S)	0.35	☐ ☐
	Liverpool CDS, m/c and handstamp as NW30.......... from	1.25(C)(S)		☐
NW30-33	Set of 4	4.00(S)	1.30	☐ ☐
N.B.	In September '84 NWPB offered for sale at £17.25 + p/p a proof sheet in colour of Series 9 cards in a limited edition of 75, each numbered and signed by the artist K. Mosley.			

		FDI	Mint
	LIVERPOOL'S ROYAL MAIL. Set of four. Prints and photos used in the Post Office exhibition at the Garden Festival. **NWPB Series 10.**		
1984, 2 MAY NW34	**LONDON-LIVERPOOL MAIL COACH 1838** **(NWPB Series 10(a))** Print 10,000 .... Liverpool CDS, Phil. Counter or 'Codesort' handstamp	 1.00(S) 1.50(C)(S)	 0.35 ☐ ☐ ☐
1984, 2 MAY NW35	**LIVERPOOL PO, CANNING DOCK 1839-1899** **(NWPB Series 10(b))** Print 10,000 .... Liverpool CDS, or handstamps as NW34	 1.00(S) 1.50(C)(S)	 0.35 ☐ ☐ ☐
1984, 2 MAY NW36	**AQUITANIA LOADING AMERICAN MAILS 1919** **(NWPB Series 10(c))** Print 10,000 .... Liverpool CDS, or handstamps as NW34	 1.00(S) 1.50(C)(S)	 0.35 ☐ ☐ ☐
1984, 2 MAY NW37	**AIRMAIL AT LIVERPOOL AERODROME, 1935** **(NWPB Series 10(d))** Print 10,000 .... Liverpool CDS, or handstamps as NW34	 1.00(S) 1.50(C)(S)	 0.35 ☐ ☐ ☐
NW34-37	Set of 4	4.00(S)	1.30 ☐ ☐
	TRAMWAYS IN THE NORTH WEST Set of four. Artist Mr. G. S. Cooper. **NWPB Series 11**		
1985, 19 AUGUST NW38	**BLACKPOOL TRAMS circa 1985 (Series 11(a))** Car 641 and 1936 streamliner Print 10,000 .... Fylde, Blackpool, Wyre 'Lancs'/3 CDS .... Blackpool Philatelic Counter Spec. handstamp .... Fylde, Blackpool 'FDI' (used in error).	 1.00(S) 1.50(C) 1.25(S) 3.00(F)	 0.25 ☐ ☐ ☐ ☐ ☐
1985, 19 AUGUST NW39	**LIVERPOOL TRAMS circa 1939 (Series 11(b)** Streamliner 155 and top covered car Print 10,000 .... Liverpool/22 CDS. .... Liverpool Philatelic Counter Spec. handstamp	 1.00(S) 1.50(C) 1.25(S)	 0.25 ☐ ☐ ☐ ☐
1985, 19 AUGUST NW40	**MANCHESTER TRAMS circa 1920 (Series 11(c))** Car 765 passing Bogie 'Balloon' car 620 Print 10,000 .... Manchester Philatelic Counter Spec. handstamp	 1.00(S) 1.25(S)	 0.25 ☐ ☐ ☐
1985, 19 AUGUST NW41	**OLDHAM TRAMS circa 1920 (Series 11(d))** Balcony car No. 4 and open top tram Print 10,000 .... Oldham/Lancs CDS. .... Oldham Philatelic Counter Spec. handstamp	 1.00(S) 1.50(C) 1.25(S)	 0.25 ☐ ☐ ☐ ☐
NW38-41	Set of 4	4.00(S)	1.00 ☐ ☐
	DISTINCTIVE POST OFFICES WITHIN NWPR Set of four. Watercolours by K. Mosley. **NWPB Series 12**		
1986, 1 SEPTEMBER NW42	**G-MEX, GREATER MANCHESTER EXHIBITION AND EVENTS CENTRE (Series 12 (A) 9.86))** Print 10,000 .... Manchester Philatelic Counter handstamp or CDS ..... from	 1.00(S) 1.25(S)(C)	 0.25 ☐ ☐ ☐
1986, 1 SEPTEMBER NW43	**PRESTON POST OFFICE, MARKET PLACE** **(Series 12(B) 9.86)** Print 10,000 .... Preston CDS.	 1.00(S) 1.50(C)	 0.25 ☐ ☐ ☐
1986, 1 SEPTEMBER NW44	**ROCHDALE POST OFFICE, THE ESPLANADE** **Series 12(C) 9.86)** Print 10,000 .... Rochdale CDS.	 1.00(S) 1.50(C)	 0.25 ☐ ☐ ☐
1986, 1 SEPTEMBER NW45	**PORT SUNLIGHT POST OFFICE (Series 12(D) 9.86)** Sub PO on Leverhulme Estate on Wirral Print 10,000 .... Liverpool or New Ferry CDS.	 1.00(S) 1.25-1.50(C)	 0.25 ☐ ☐ ☐
N.B.	A cachet – Map of NW Postal Region, was applied at Manchester to first day of sale cards.		
NW42-45	Set of 4	4.00(S)	1.00 ☐ ☐

PROMOTIONAL, PUBLICITY AND POSTCODE CARDS

			FDI	Mint	
1983, — MAY		**GPO 3 MOBILE POST OFFICE.** Photograph of vehicle refurbished 1982.			
NWP1		Reverse headed 'POSTCODES'. **(NWPB PR1)**			
(1) 1983, — May		1st Print 2,000 (Reverse off white matt surface)	—	2.00	☐
(2) 1983, — August		2nd Print 2,000 (Reverse white shiny surface)	—	2.25	☐
1983, — MAY		**AUSTIN SEVEN VAN DGH 327.** Photograph of 1936 refurbished van in Toad Lane, Rochdale.			
NWP2		Reverse headed 'POSTCODES'. **(NWPB PR2)**			
(1) 1983, — May		1st Print 2,000 (Reverse off white matt surface)	—	1.75	☐
(2) 1983, — August		2nd Print 2,000 (Reverse white shiny surface)	—	2.00	☐

NW1

NW2

NW5

NW3

NW7

NW8

NW12

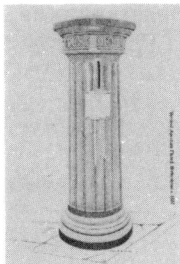
NW13

NW20

NW22

NW37

NW30

NW40

NW45

STAMP MAGAZINE

BRITAIN'S LEADING STAMP PUBLICATION

STAMP MAGAZINE — Established for over 50 years — is the most popular and widely read Philatelic magazine in the U.K.
Packed with adverts and features, it provides everything the collector needs every month. Regular topics include all the latest information on Covers and Cancellations, Postcards, Auction News, Stamp Fairs, Exhibitions, Postal History, Thematics, G.B., a thorough world New Issue guide plus Crown Agents News; even advice for beginners and much, much more . . .

Order a regular copy each month, £1.00 from your local newsagent or, if you prefer, take an annual subscription, £12.00 U.K. (postage free) or £20.50 overseas (surface mail).

THROUGHOUT THE YEAR

you will keep referring to BRITISH STAMP VALUES A bargain at only £2.95, it provides a priced catalogue of the stamps of Great Britain, Channel Islands and the Isle of Man, with first day covers, presentation packs, stamp booklets and PHQ cards. There is a separate section listing the British 'Regional' postcards. Everything for the G.B. enthusiast in one handy volume.

Get a copy now from your Newsagent or direct from the address below.

Link House Magazines Ltd, Dingwall Avenue, Croydon, CR9 2TA

SOUTH EASTERN POSTAL REGION

Cards can be obtained from:

Philatelic Counter
51 Ship Street
BRIGHTON BN1 1AA

Philatelic Counter
28 High Street
CANTERBURY CT1 1AA

Philatelic Counter
North Street
GUILDFORD GU1 1AA

Philatelic Counter
Slindon Street
PORTSMOUTH PO1 1AA

Philatelic Counter
38/39 Peascod Street
WINDSOR SL4 1AA

South Eastern Postal Board (to 30 Sept. '86)
Milton House,
Churchill Square,
BRIGHTON BN1 2EQ

		FDI	Mint		

1973, 2 AUGUST — **DORKING POSTBUS** (One view)
SE1
No border
(1) 1973, 2 August — 1st Print 7,500 .... 31.00(S) 21.00 ☐ ☐
Four reverse typesettings known —
  1. Blue cast. FDI and Mint values above
  2. Blue cast — damaged 'C' in POST CARD'
     FDI £29. Mint £30
  3. Orange cast — small fine lower right Mint £2.75
  4. Green cast — no line at right Mint £19
Trial print also known — placed on sale — Reverse with large
'MK' 26mm long at top left Mint £47
(2) 1978, 1 September — 2nd Print 5,000 (Ref. RCC1 1978 Reprint) .... 2.25(C) 1.00 ☐ ☐

1973, 3 SEPTEMBER — **FARNHAM POST OFFICE MURAL (PO1)**
SE2
Shows pictures of the Mural at Farnham Post Office
(1) 1973, 3 September — 1st Print 3,000 (Lower picture has several cars in view)...... — 1.50 ☐
(2) 1978, 8 August — 2nd Print 6,000 (Lower picture has no cars in view).......... — 1.00 ☐

N.B. Mural Description card (140mm x 74mm). Issued with first sales of 1st print cards £12.50.

1973, 24 SEPTEMBER — **OXTED-LINGFIELD POSTBUS**
SE3
Shows Postbus at Crowhurst
(1) 1973, 24 September — 1st Print 5,800 .... 30.00(S) 2.00 ☐ ☐
Two reverse typesettings known —
  1. 'MURRAY KING' under 'S' of 'POST CARD'
  2. 'MURRAY KING' under 'ST' of 'POST CARD' and broken 'B'
     in 'PUBLISHED'
(2) 1978, 1 September — 2nd Print 5,000 (Ref. RCC2 1978 Reprint) .... 2.50(C) 1.00 ☐ ☐

1973, 22 OCTOBER — **LOADING MAIL AT GATWICK AIRPORT**
SE4
To BAC111 Jet
(1) 1973, 22 October — 1st Print 6,000 .... — 2.00 ☐
(2) 1978, 1 September — 2nd Print 8,000 (Ref. RCC3 1978 Reprint) .... 2.00(C) 1.00 ☐ ☐
Two reverse typesettings known for both prints.

1974, — MARCH — **CANTERBURY-CRUNDALE POSTBUS (PO2)**
SE5
4 views of places on postbus route
(1) 1974, — March — 1st print 3,000 (Captions on top left reverse of card).......... — 3.75 ☐
(2) 1978, 16 June — 2nd Print 6,600 (Captions over each view on front of card)... 3.75(C) 1.00 ☐ ☐

N.B. All cards both (1) and (2) have a cachet applied to the reverse "Carried on the Canterbury postbus" in violet.

1974, 4 MARCH — **SITTINGBOURNE POSTBUS AT SHELL LABORATORIES**
SE6
One view
Print 2,500 .... 25.00(C) 12.50 ☐ ☐
Trial print also known — placed on sale —
Reverse with 'Photograph by Stephen Wheeler, Sittingbourne'
vertical to right of 'EXCLUSIVELY----6303', FDI and Mint
£105.

N.B. FDI of both prints normally have Postbus dated cachet applied in violet.

1974, 4 MARCH — **SITTINGBOURNE POSTBUS AT WORMSHILL POST OFFICE**
SE7
One view
(1) 1974, 4 March — 1st Print 2,500 (Last line of description reverse ends
"Wormshill").. 40.00(C) 40.00 ☐ ☐
Trial print also known — placed on sale —
Reverse with 'Photograph by Stephen Wheeler' etc as SE6 trial
print, Mint £105.
(2) 1978, 1 November — 2nd Print 5,000 (Last line of description on reverse ends
"March 4, 1975") small 'MK' top left .... 2.50(C) 1.75 ☐ ☐

N.B. FDI of all prints normally have Postbus dated cachet applied in violet. 2nd Print also known with cachet for 5th anniversary.

		FDI	Mint	
1974, 30 MARCH SE8	**TUNBRIDGE WELLS POSTBUS AT WADHURST** One view of Postbus OUF 269M facing towards right side of card (uncoded)			
(1) 1974, 30 March	1st Print 1,000 (Matt surface on picture side)...............	105.00(S)	13.00	☐ ☐
(2) 1978, 14 May	2nd Print 2,000 (Glazed surface on picture side)............	—	2.25	☐
1974, 30 MARCH SE9	**TUNBRIDGE WELLS POSTBUS AT MAYFIELD** One view of Postbus OUF 269M facing towards left side of card (uncoded)			
(1) 1974, 30 March	1st Print 1,000 (Matt surface on picture side)...............	105.00(C)	8.00	☐ ☐
(2) 1978, 14 May	2nd Print 2,000 (Glazed surface on picture side)............	—	2.25	☐

1974, 1 JULY
 SE10
	HUNGERFORD POSTBUS (Uncoded)
	 Shown at Denford Mill House, One view, no border
	 Print 5,000...
	 Two reverse typesettings known —
	   Vertical print ending '6303'
	   1. close to 'T' in 'POST CARD'
	   2. towards centre of 'T C' in 'POST CARD'
		10.00(S)	5.00	☐ ☐

1976, 28 APRIL SE11	**NEWBURY POSTBUS** Five views. Centre view is circular.			
(1) 1976, 28 April	1st Print 5,000 (Uncoded)..................................	8.00(F)	8.50	☐ ☐
(2) 1978, 2 October	2nd Print 5,000 (Ref. SEPR2/1 and has MK symbol top left on reverse)...	1.50(C)	1.50	☐ ☐
1978, — SEPTEMBER SE12	**BRIGHTON CENTRE POST OFFICE** View of the Brighton Centre on promenade			
(1) 1978, — September	1st Print 5,000 (Ref. SPW5MS78)...........................	—	1.75	☐
(2) 1979, 12 February	2nd Print 5,000 'G' Girobank symbol added to wording above view on front.(Uncoded)......................................	2.50(C)	0.50	☐ ☐
N.B.	Both known with Brighton special handstamps from November 1978 — From £3.			
1978, 2 OCTOBER SE13	**HUNGERFORD POSTBUS** Five views. Black border.			
(1) 1978, 2 October	1st Print 6,500 (Ref. SEPR2/1).............................	1.50(C)	1.50	☐ ☐
(2) 1979, 9 April	2nd Print 12,650 (Ref. SEPR8/2)...........................	1.25(C)	1.00	☐ ☐
1978, 2 OCTOBER SE14	**HENLEY ON THAMES POSTBUS** Five views. Black border.			
(1) 1978, 2 October	1st Print 6,500 (Ref. SEPR2/1).............................	1.50(C)	1.50	☐ ☐
(2) 1979, 9 April	2nd Print 12,650 (Ref. SEPR17/2)..........................	1.25(C)	1.00	☐ ☐
1978, 1 DECEMBER SE15	**TUNBRIDGE WELLS POSTBUS IN COUNTRY** Shown in front of cottage. Print 15,000... Tunbridge Wells oval postbus handstamp in violet...........	2.60(C) 4.00(C)	1.00	☐ ☐ ☐
1979, 9 APRIL SE16	**NEWBURY POSTBUS (SEPR15/16/1)** Five views, black border, centre view is square. Print 12,650	1.50(C)	1.00	☐ ☐
N.B.	Known with local cancels for 4th and 5th anniversaries.			
1979, 1 OCTOBER SE17	**REDHILL-OUTWOOD POSTBUS (SEPR 18/1)** Shown by the Old Mill Windmill, Outwood			
(1) 1979, 1 October	1st Print 5,000 (Guillotined from the back).................	5.25(C)	1.30	☐ ☐
N.B.	1,200 of these cards were printed with a Post Office cachet "Posted on first day of Redhill-Outwood Postbus". Most of these overprinted cards were used on the first day. FDI £5, Mint £50.			
(2) 1979, — November	2nd Print 7,500 (Guillotined from the front)	1.20(C)	0.75	☐ ☐
N.B.	FDI backdated to 1 October 1979.			
1980, 7 MAY SE18	**BRIGHTON LANDMARKS** Shows three points of interest with Brighton Pier in the background. Print 10,000 .... Brighton/East Sussex 'FDI'...................................	1.75(C) 1.50(F)	1.00	☐ ☐ ☐
	KENT/HAMPSHIRE/ISLE OF WIGHT POSTBUSES — Set of 9 with information folder. Single views with black border.			

			FDI	Mint	

1970, 7 JULY
SE19
CANTERBURY-CRUNDALE POSTBUS (SEPR1)
Shown at the City Wall, Canterbury.
Print 20,000 .... 1.00(S) 0.30 ☐ ☐
Brighton/East Sussex CDS................................. 1.20(C) ☐
Canterbury m/c slogan or Godmersham/Canterbury CDS ... 2.75(C) ☐

1980, 7 JULY
SE20
PETWORTH-BIGNOR POSTBUS (SEPR4)
Sutton Village
Print 20,000 .... 1.00(S) 0.30 ☐ ☐
Brighton/East Sussex CDS................................. 1.20(C) ☐
Petworth/West Sussex CDS or m/c slogan .... 3.75(C) ☐

1980, 7 JULY
SE21
SITTINGBOURNE-WORMSHILL POSTBUS (SEPR5)
Milstead Village.
Print 20,000 .... 1.00(S) 0.30 ☐ ☐
Brighton/East Sussex CDS................................. 1.30(C) ☐
Sittingbourne/Kent CDS + cachet......................... 2.75(C) ☐

1980, 7 JULY
SE22
TUNBRIDGE WELLS-MAYFIELD POSTBUS (SEPR6)
Mayfield High Street.
Print 20,000 .... 1.00(S) 0.30 ☐ ☐
Brighton/East Sussex CDS................................. 1.20(C) ☐
Tunbridge Wells/Kent CDS + cachet...................... 3.00(C) ☐

1980, 7 JULY
SE23
HEATHFIELD-WALDRON POSTBUS (SEPR7)
The Starr Inn, Waldron.
Print 20,000 .... 1.00(S) 0.30 ☐ ☐
Brighton/East Sussex CDS................................. 1.20(C) ☐
Heathfield m/c or Tunbridge Wells CDS .... 2.50(C) ☐

1980, 7 JULY
SE24
HAILSHAM-BODLE STRET GREEN POSTBUS (SEPR11)
The Byeway, Bodle Street Green.
Print 20,000 .... 1.00(S) 0.30 ☐ ☐
Brighton/East Sussex CDS................................. 1.20(C) ☐
Sussex Coast CDS... 2.25(C) ☐

1980, 7 JULY
SE25
NEWPORT-NEWTOWN POSTBUS (SEPR12)
Carisbrooke Castle, I.O.W.
Print 20,000 .... 1.00(S) 0.30 ☐ ☐
Brighton CDS or Isle of Wight /A or B m/c + cachet .... 1.00-2.00(C) ☐
Newport/I.O.W. CDS .... 3.00(C) ☐

1980, 7 JULY
SE26
NEWPORT-BRIGHTSTONE POSTBUS (SEPR13)
Climbing Berry Lane, Chillerton I.O.W.
Print 20,000 .... 1.00(S) 0.30 ☐ ☐
Brighton CDS or Isle of Wight/A or B m/c + cachet .... 1.20-2.00(C) ☐
Newport/I.O.W. CDS .... 3.00(C) ☐

1980, 7 JULY
SE27
PETERSFIELD-FROXFIELD POSTBUS (SEPR14)
Froxfield Green.
Print 20,000 .... 1.00(S) 0.30 ☐ ☐
Brighton/East Sussex CDS................................. 1.20(C) ☐
Petersfield Hants/9 CDS + cachet .... 3.00(C) ☐

SE19-27
Set of 9 as above issued with red information folder .... 7.50(C) 2.25 ☐ ☐

BERKSHIRE/OXFORDSHIRE/SURREY POSTBUSES
Set of 9 with information folder. Single views with black border.

1980, 6 OCTOBER
SE28
DORKING-OCKLEY POSTBUS (SEPR2)
White House, Coldharbour.
Print 20,000 .... 1.00(S) 0.30 ☐ ☐
Brighton/East Sussex CDS or Redhill m/c.................... 1.20-1.75(C) ☐
Reigate & Redhill/Surrey RH1 1AA CDS..................... 2.50(C) ☐

1980, 6 OCTOBER
SE29
OXTED-LINGFIELD POSTBUS (SEPR3)
Crowhurst Place, Lingfield.
Print 20,000 .... 1.00(S) 0.30 ☐ ☐
Brighton CDS, Redhill m/c or Reigate & Redhill CDS......... 1.20-2.00(C) ☐
Oxted CDS or Lingfield CDS .... 5.00(C) ☐

1980, 6 OCTOBER
SE30
HUNGERFORD-EAST GARSTON POSTBUS (SEPR8)
East Garston.
Print 20,000 .... 1.00(S) 0.30 ☐ ☐
Brighton CDS, Newbury/Berks m/c.......................... 1.20-1.75(C) ☐
East Garston/Newbury CDS................................. 3.00(C) ☐

		FDI	Mint

1980, 6 OCTOBER
SE31
HUNGERFORD-GREAT SHEFFORD (SEPR 9)
Denford Mill.
Print 20,000 .... 1.00(S) 0.30 ☐ ☐
Brighton CDS or Newbury/Berks m/c........................ 1.20-1.80(C) ☐
Great Shefford/Newbury, Berks CDS...................... 5.00(C) ☐

1980, 6 OCTOBER
SE32
HUNGERFORD-KINTBURY POSTBUS (SEPR10)
Kintbury Level Crossing.
Print 20,000 .... 1.00(S) 0.30 ☐ ☐
Brighton CDS or Newbury/Berks m/c........................ 1.20-1.75(C) ☐

1980, 6 OCTOBER
SE33
NEWBURY-WEST ILSLEY POSTBUS (SEPR15)
Donnington Castle.
Print 20,000 .... 1.00(S) 0.30 ☐ ☐
Brighton CDS or Newbury/Berks m/c........................ 1.20-1.75(C) ☐

1980, 6 OCTOBER
SE34
NEWBURY-CHADDLEWORTH POSTBUS (SEPR16)
North Heath.
Print 20,000 .... 1.00(S) 0.30 ☐ ☐
Brighton CDS or Newbury/Berks m/c........................ 1.20-1.75(C) ☐
Chaddleworth/Newbury. Berks CDS......................... 5.00(C) ☐

1980, 6 OCTOBER
SE35
HENLEY ON THAMES-FREITH POSTBUS (SEPR17)
Hambleden Village.
Print 20,000 .... 1.00(S) 0.30 ☐ ☐
Brighton CDS or Reading/Berks CDS .... 1.20-1.75(C) ☐

1980, 6 OCTOBER
SE36
REDHILL-OUTWOOD POSTBUS (SEPR18/2)
The Old Mill, Outwood.
Print 20,000 .... 1.00(S) 0.30 ☐ ☐
Brighton CDS; Redhill m/c or Reigate & Redhill CDS .... 1.20-2.50(C) ☐

SE28-36 Set of 9 as above issued with red information folder......... 7.50(S) 2.25 ☐ ☐

1981, 25 MAY
SE37
(1) 1981, 25 May
(2) 1981, 29 June
WORLD'S FIRST SCHEDULED HOVERMAIL (SEPR19)
Isle of Wight - Portsmouth.
1st Print 10,000 (Ref. SEPR 19 May 1981) .... 1.50(S) 0.75 ☐ ☐
2nd Print 5,000 (Ref. SEPR19/2 June 1981)
Brighton/East Sussex CDS.................................. 10.00(C) 0.30 ☐ ☐
Brighton/BN1 1AA large s.ring CDS .... 10.00(C) ☐
(Also known with this cancel 22 JUNE)

1981, 21 OCTOBER
SE38
GUILDFORD HEAD POST OFFICE (SEPR20)
Drawing of building. Philatelic Counter opening.
Print 10,000 .... 1.20(S) 0.30 ☐ ☐
Guildford/Surrey CDS or m/c slogan .... 1.75(C) ☐

POST OFFICE HISTORICAL TRANSPORT — SET 1
Set of 3 in a red card wallet.

1982, 22 FEBRUARY
SE39
FIVE WHEELED CENTRE CYCLE (SEPR22)
Print 10,000 .... 1.20(S) 0.35 ☐ ☐
Brighton/East Sussex CDS or Horsham/West Sussex CDS .... 1.75(C) ☐

1982, 22 FEBRUARY
SE40
DOVER-LONDON STAGE COACH NO. 1058 (SEPR23)
Print 10,000 .... 1.20(S) 0.35 ☐ ☐
Brighton/East Sussex CDS, Dover/Kent CDS or London (S) 1.20-1.75(C)(S) ☐

1982, 22 FEBRUARY
SE41
MORRIS COMMERCIAL VAN (SEPR24)
Print 10,000 .... 1.20(S) 0.35 ☐ ☐
Brighton/East Sussex CDS.................................. 1.20(C) ☐

SE39-41 Set of 3 as above in red card wallet .... 3.50(S) 1.00 ☐ ☐

1982, 24 FEBRUARY
SE42
OPENING PORTSMOUTH PHILATELIC COUNTER (SEPR21)
Print 10,000 .... 2.50(S) 2.00 ☐ ☐
Portsmouth 'FDI' on Regional definitive..................... 2.50(F) ☐
Portsmouth & Isle of Wight CDS or Portsmouth/Hants CDS .... 2.75(C) ☐

N.B. Known FDI used with HMS Victory cachets.
Known overprinted by Nat. Postal Museum for Mary Rose Philatelic Appeal donation receipts.

SE1

SE12(1)

SE13

SE18

SE20

SE37

SE38

SE45

SE50

SE56

SE59

SE62

SE65

SE67

SE68

		FDI	Mint	
	POST OFFICE HISTORICAL TRANSPORT — SET 2 Set of 3 in a red card wallet.			
1982, 19 APRIL SE43	**ROYAL MAIL AIR SERVICE (SEPR25)** Print 10,000 .... Croydon, Surrey CDS or Reigate & Redhill/Surrey CDS......	1.00(S) 1.75(C)	0.35	☐ ☐ ☐
1982, 19 APRIL SE44	**FORD AA MAIL VAN (SEPR26)** Print 10,000 .... Romford CDS or Sittingbourne/Kent CDS	1.00(S) 1.50(C)	0.35	☐ ☐ ☐
1982, 19 APRIL SE45	**MORRIS COMMERCIAL 30CWT VAN (SEPR27)** Print 10,000 .... Brighton/East Sussex CDS...	1.00(S) 1.25(C)	0.35	☐ ☐ ☐
SE43-45	Set of 3 as above in red card wallet	3.00(S)	1.00	☐ ☐
1982, 6 MAY SE46	**WINDSOR POST OFFICE PHILATELIC COUNTER 1982** Issued on opening day of counter. **(SEPR28)** Print 10,000	2.20(S)	1.60	☐ ☐
N.B.	Most were printed on smooth white card. Known also on rough off white card.			
1982, 19 JULY SE47	**POST OFFICE HISTORICAL TRANSPORT — SET 3** Set of 3 in a red card wallet. **PARCEL MAIL SERVICE TO BRIGHTON 1887 (SEPR29)** Print 10,000 .... Brighton/East Sussex CDS...	1.00(S) 1.25(C)	0.35	☐ ☐ ☐
1982, 19 JULY SE48	**CORONATION AERIAL POST 1911 (SEPR30)** Print 10,000 .... Windsor 'Castle' Philatelic Special handstamp...............	1.00(S) 1.25(S)	0.35	☐ ☐ ☐
1982, 19 JULY SE49	**BASKET CARRIER TRICYCLE, READING 1897 (SEPR31)** Print 10,000 .... Reading/Berks CDS	1.00(S) 1.50(C)	0.35	☐ ☐ ☐
SE47-49	Set of 3 as above in red card wallet	3.00(S)	1.00	☐ ☐
1982, 13 SEPTEMBER SE50	**BRIGHTON BANDSTAND (SEPR35)** Philatelic Counter 10th Anniversary. Print 10,000 .... Brighton/East Sussex CDS or Brighton/BN1 1AA CDS ...... Lewes/East Sussex CDS...	1.00(S) 1.50(C) 1.75(C)	0.30	☐ ☐ ☐ ☐
	POST OFFICE HISTORICAL TRANSPORT — SET 4 Set of 3 in red card wallet.			
1982, 18 OCTOBER SE51	**DAIMLER MOTOR VAN, READING-NEWBURY 1898 (SEPR32)** Print 10,000 .... Newbury/Berks CDS..	1.00(S) 1.50(C)	0.35	☐ ☐ ☐
1982, 18 OCTOBER SE52	**PARCEL POST MOTOR COACH 1905 (SEPR33)** Print 10,000 .... Brighton/East Sussex CDS...	1.00(S) 1.25(C)	0.35	☐ ☐ ☐
1982, 18 OCTOBER SE53	**EXPERIMENTAL POST CAR, SITTINGBOURNE 1905 (SEPR34)** Print 10,000 .... Sittingbourne/Kent CDS	1.00(S) 1.50(C)	0.35	☐ ☐ ☐
SE51-53	Set of 3 as above in red card wallet	3.00(S)	1.00	☐ ☐
1983, 18 JULY SE54	**CARTOONS — SET 1** Reproduced by kind permission of Punch. **'WRONG ADDRESS, MATE! — WIMPEY SITE (SEPR36)** Print 10,000 .... Sussex Coast CDS...	1.00(S) 1.25(C)	0.30	☐ ☐ ☐
1983, 18 JULY SE55	**'BEWARE OF THE BOG' (SEPR37)** Print 10,000 .... Brighton/East Sussex CDS...	1.00(S) 1.25(C)	0.30	☐ ☐ ☐
SE54-55	Set of 2	2.00(S)	0.60	☐ ☐
	CARTOONS — SET 2 Reproduced by kind permission of Punch.			
1983, 19 SEPTEMBER SE56	**'NOISY DOG BUT HARMLESS' (SEPR38)** Print 10,000 .... Sussex Coast CDS...	1.00(S) 1.25(C)	0.30	☐ ☐ ☐

		FDI	Mint

1983, 19 SEPTEMBER 'ACE PRIVATE POSTAL SERVICE' (SEPR39)
SE57 Print 10,000 .... 1.00(S) 0.30 ☐ ☐
      Lewes/East Sussex CDS or Brighton/East Sussex CDS ..... 1.25(C)   ☐

SE56-57 Set of 2 .... 2.00(S) 0.60 ☐ ☐

1984
N.B. In April 500 packs of five local scene postcards went on sale at the Philatelic Counter and Crown POs in Guildford which were not officially published by SEPR. All were black and white drawings by Shirley Veater, hand painted (red postvan, postbox, etc.) of:-
THE GUILDHALL, GUILDFORD   WOOL LANE, MIDHURST
THE CASTLE GATEWAY, GUILDFORD   ABINGER HAMMER
THE OLD TOWN HALL, GODALMING

Similar local views and humourous designs have been used for Christmas cards, plain folded cards and letter sheets sold over the Guildford Philatelic Counter.

1984, 7 JUNE — **THE OSTRICH, COLNBROOK (SEPR40)**
SE58 Mailcoach outside the Inn — as in 1784.
      Print 10,000 .... 1.00(S) 0.35 ☐ ☐
      Haywards Heath/West Sussex CDS........................ 1.50(C)   ☐
      8 or 9 JUNE '84 Haywards Heath handstamp — as 7 JUNE but without 'First day of sale' .... 0.75(S)   ☐

N.B. Known with 7 JUNE handstamp and PO cachet 'Carried on the mailcoach and autographed by driver JOHN PARKER' with his signature in black ink £2.50.

1984, 10 JULY — **THE GEORGE HOTEL, READING (SEPR41)**
SE59 Mailcoach outside the Hotel — as in 1784.
      Print 10,000 .... 1.00(S) 0.35 ☐ ☐
      Reading/Berks m/c slogan................................ 1.25(C)   ☐

N.B. In September and December London scene postcards went on sale at Gatwick Airport Crown PO. Both were black and white drawings by Shirley Veater (with red postbox, bus, etc.) inscribed 'HAVE ARRIVED SAFELY LONDON/GATWICK'. These were not published by SEPR nor exclusively sold at Gatwick PO.

1984, 30 OCTOBER — **THE BRIGHTON DAY MAILS (SEPR42)**
SE60 Passing over Hookwood Common
      Print 10,000 .... 1.00(S) 0.35 ☐ ☐
      Brighton/East Sussex CDS................................. 1.25(C)   ☐

1984, 30 OCTOBER — **A LONDON MAIL AND STAGE COACH (SEPR43)**
SE61 At an Inn, probably on the main Dover road
      Print 10,000 .... 1.00(S) 0.35 ☐ ☐
      Brighton CDS or Dover/Kent CDS......................... 1.25(C)   ☐

1985, 30 JULY — **POSTBOXES IN WINDSOR AND MAIDENHEAD (SEPR44)**
SE62 To mark 350 years of Royal Mail Service
      Print 12,000 .... 1.00(S) 0.35 ☐ ☐
      Maidenhead/Berks CDS .... 1.25(C)   ☐

1985, 30 JULY — **POST OFFICE TRANSPORT DISPLAY AT BAGSHOT PARK (SEPR45)**
SE63 In commemoration of signing of Royal Proclamation at Bagshot in 1635
      Print 12,000 .... 1.00(S) 0.35 ☐ ☐
      Bagshot/Surrey CDS, NPM '350 years' or other handstamp 1.25(S)   ☐
                                                              to 4.00(C)

1985, 7 OCTOBER — **BRIGHTON TRANSORMA ANNIVERSARY (SEPR46)**
SE64 50th anniversary of introduction of sorting equipment at Brighton in 1935
      Print 8,000... 1.00(S0 0.35 ☐ ☐
      Sussex Coast, Brighton/East Sussex CDS or Brighton Phil.
      Counter Special handstamp................................. 1.25   ☐
                                                              to 1.50(C)(S)

1985, 6 DECEMBER — **CANTERBURY SORTING OFFICE (SEPR47)**
SE65 New mechanised Letter Office opened Dec. 1985, inset – view of Canterbury Cathedral.
      Print 9,500... 1.00(S) 0.35 ☐ ☐
      Canterbury CDS, m/c or Phil. Counter handstamp .... 1.50(C)(S)   ☐

		FDI	Mint
1986, 18 FEBRUARY SE66	**ROYAL GREENWICH OBSERVATORY (SEPR48)** The Observatory at Herstmonceux Castle, Hailsham, inset – Halley's Comet in 1910. Print 12,000 .... Sussex Coast CDS, Brighton Phil. Counter handstamp, Brighton/East Sussex CDS, Hailsham CDS or Tunbridge Wells 'Opening of Fiveways stamp shop' handstamp	1.00(S) 1.25 to 2.00(C)(S)	0.50 ☐ ☐ ☐
1986, 9 SEPTEMBER SE67	**FIRST AERIAL POST, HENDON-WINDSOR (SEPR49)** Gustav Hamel in his Bleriot monoplane, inset – Blue Airmail Pillar Box. Print 12,000 .... Hendon; NWDO CDS or Windsor m/c	1.00(S) from 1.30(C)	0.25 ☐ ☐ ☐
1986, 30 SEPTEMBER SE68	**FIRST POST OFFICE ON WHEELS – GPO 1 (SEPR50)** First Mobile PO inaugurated Sept. 1936, inset – Postmaster General handing in first telegram. Print 12,000 .... Tonbridge CDS	1.00(S) 1.30(C)	0.25 ☐ ☐ ☐

N.B. A cachet – 'SEPR50 The last postcard published in the South East Postal Region' – was applied to most FDI cards at Tonbridge.

SW1

SW8

SW10

SW12

SW15

SW19

SW22

SW25

SW27

SW29

SW30

SW31

SOUTH WESTERN POSTAL REGION

Cards can be obtained from:

Philatelic Counter
New Bond Street
BATH BA1 1AA

Philatelic Counter
Post Office Road
BOURNEMOUTH BH1 1AA

Philatelic Counter
Merchant Street
BRISTOL BS1 3EJ

Philatelic Sales
HPO Counter
Bridport Road
DORCHESTER DT1 1AA

Philatelic Counter
Bedford Street
EXETER EX1 1AA

Philatelic Counter
Kings Square
GLOUCESTER GL1 1AD

Philatelic Counter
5 St. Andrew's Cross
PLYMOUTH PL1 1AB

Philatelic Sales
HPO Counter
24 Castle Street
SALISBURY SP1 1AA

Philatelic Counter
57 High Street
SOUTHAMPTON SO9 1AA

Philatelic Counter
Civic Centre
Theatre Square
SWINDON SN1 1QW

Philatelic Sales
HPO Counter
38 North Street
TAUNTON TA1 1AA

Philatelic Counter
Fleet Street
TORQUAY TQ1 1AA

Philatelic Counter
High Cross
TRURO TR1 2AP

South Western Postal Board (to 30 Sept. '86)
Mercury House
Bond Street
BRISTOL BS1 3PD

		FDI	Mint	
1971, 18 OCTOBER SW1	**DORCHESTER MURAL** Shows various pictures of mural at Dorchester.			
(1) 1971, 18 October	1st Print 30,000 (Smooth white card).......................	5.00(S)	1.50	☐ ☐
(2) 1978, 15 June	2nd Print 22,000 (Rough off-white card)....................	—	0.30	☐
N.B.	1st Print also known used on creamy/white card — £6.00 FDI.			
1972, 24 JULY SW2	**WEYMOUTH MURAL** Shows pictures of mural at Weymouth Post Office.			
(1) 1972, 24 July	1st Print 15,000 (Smooth white card).......................	120.00(C)	1.00	☐ ☐
(2) 1978, 15 June	2nd Print 22,000 (Rough off-white card)....................	—	0.30	☐
1973, 25 APRIL SW3	**RALPH ALLEN** Portrait of Ralph Allen, Bath Postmaster.			
(1) 1973, 25 April	1st Print 2,000 (Caption: "Ralph Allen after Hudson")........	15.00(S)	4.50	☐ ☐
(2) 1973, April	2nd Print 13,000 (Caption: "Ralph Allen (gap) Studio of Thomas Hudson")...	—	1.00	☐
(3) 1973, July	3rd Print 10,000 (Caption: "Ralph Allen Studio of Thomas Hudson") (No gap)......................................	—	0.90	☐
(4) 1978, 20 November	4th Print 1,500 Est. (Caption as SW3(1) but envelope in stamp box has pointed flap)..	—	4.00	☐
N.B.	Withdrawn after 3 days as original wording had been used in error but stock had not been destroyed and more turned up later (a few were even sold in 1982 and 1983).			
(5) 1979, 9 April	5th Print 10,000 (Caption as SW3(3) but envelope in stamp box has pointed flap)..	—	0.30	☐
1973, 25 APRIL SW4	**BATH MAIL COACH** (Normal size) John Palmer's Mail Coach.			
(1) 1973, 25 April	1st Print 10,000 (Vertical print on reverse under C of Post Card)..	15.00(C)	20.00	☐ ☐
	Two reverse typesettings known — '3' of '1973' 1. under 'n' in 'and' FDI and Mint as above 2. under 'd' in 'and' FDI £10, Mint £5			
(2) 1973, July	2nd Print 60,000 (Vertical print of reverse under OS or Post Card)..	—	0.25	☐
1973, JULY SW5	**BATH MAIL COACH** (Jumbo size) John Palmer's Mail Coach.			
(1) 1973, July	1st Print 10,000 (204mm x 149mm).........................	—	1.00	☐
(2) 1978, June	2nd Print 11,000 (205mm x 148mm).........................	—	1.00	☐
(3) 1978, December	3rd Print 20,000 (203mm x 150mm).........................	—	0.45	☐
1974, 1 JULY SW6	**WEST COUNTRY MAILS, PICCADILLY** (SWPR2) Painting by James Pollard.			
(1) 1974, 1 July	1st Print 20,000 ("Postcard" 18mm long)....................	—	1.50	☐
(2) 1974, 1 July	2nd Print 5,000 ("Postcard" 27mm long)............ 50.00	-120.00(C)	5.00	☐ ☐
(3) 1977, December	3rd Print 10,000 ("Postcard" 24mm long)...................	—	0.25	☐
(4) 1978, June	4th Print 30,000. Identical to 3rd Print.....................	—	0.25	☐
1974, 1 JULY SW7	**EXETER MAIL COACH, WINTERSLOW** (SWPR3) Painting by R. Havell.			
(1) 1974, 1 July	1st Print 20,000 ("Postcard" 18mm long)....................	—	1.50	☐
(2) 1974, 1 July	2nd print 5,000 ("Postcard" 27mm long)............. 50.00	-120.00(C)	5.00	☐ ☐
(3) 1977, December	3rd Print 10,000 ("Postcard" 24mm long)...................	—	0.25	☐
(4) 1978, June	4th Print 30,000. Identical to 3rd Print.....................	—	0.25	☐

			FDI	Mint	
1974, 1 JULY	**RUSSELLS' WAGGON 1833 (SWPR4)**	Falmouth to London.			
SW8					
(1) 1974, 1 July	1st Print 20,000 ("Postcard" 18mm long)...................		—	1.50	☐
(2) 1974, 1 July	2nd print 5,000 ("Postcard" 27mm long)............... 50.00		-120.00(C)	29.00	☐ ☐
(3) 1974, July	3rd Print 5,000 ("Postcard" 24mm long, rounded flap to envelope in stamp box).....................................		—	6.00	☐
(4) 1977 December	4th Print 10,000 ("Postcard" 24mm long, pointed flap to envelope in stamp box).....................................		—	0.25	☐
(5) 1978, June	5th Print 30,000. Identical to 4th Print.....................		—	0.25	☐
1978, 17 MAY	**BARNES CROSS POSTBOX (SWPR5)**	Also shows a postman in period uniform.			
SW9					
(1) 1978, 17 May	1st Print 40,000 (Shiny surface)............................		2.00(S)	0.75	☐ ☐
(2) 1979, May	2nd Print 20,000 (Matt surface).............................		—	0.30	☐
1978, 20 SEPTEMBER	**HONITON-LUPPITT POSTBUS (SWPR6)**	Shown at Dunkeswell Post Office.			
SW10					
(1) 1978, 20 September	1st Print 40,000 (Shiny surface)............................		1.60(S)	0.75	☐ ☐
	Honiton/Devon CDS + Postbus ticket cachet 'Honiton Postbus/The First in England'.............................		5.00(C)		☐
	Known also used 23 OCT '79 on 12th anniversary first Postbus service in England.				
20 September	PRESENTATION PACK — Postbus post card, tickets, timetable and descriptive sheet — in folder Print 7,000..		—	7.50	☐
(2) 1979, November	2nd Print 20,000 (Matt surface).............................		—	0.30	☐
1979, 17 APRIL	**POSTAL SERVICES IN CORNWALL (SWPR7)**	4 Views.			
SW11					
(1) 1979, 17 April	1st Print 40,000 (Bright print)...............................		1.50(S)	0.75	☐ ☐
	St. Mawes/Truro or St. Marys/Scilly CDS..................		2.25(C)		☐
(2) 1979, June	2nd print 40,000 (Colours lighter)...........................		—	0.30	☐
1979, 26 NOVEMBER	**MAIL TRAINS OF THE SOUTH WEST** (Normal size) **(SWPR8)**	4 Views of locomotives.			
SW12					
	Print 50,000..		1.50(S)	0.30	☐ ☐
	Swindon/Wilts CDS; Great Western TPO CDS............... 1.75-2.75(C)				☐
N.B.	FDI (S) known with or without cachet 'AIR DROPPED AT SOUTH MARSTON AIRFIELD' etc in black with additional flown cachet and Captain's signature — £2.00.				
	Exists (i) Reverse black print on white card				
	(ii) Reverse grey/black on white card				
	(iii) Reverse black print on creamy white card.				
1980, 12 MARCH	**MAIL TRAINS OF THE SOUTH WEST** (Jumbo size) **(SWPR8 Jumbo)**	4 Views of Locomotives.			
SW13					
(1) 1980, 12 March	1st Print 5,000 (Small nick in stem of R in "Trains" on the front)..		3.00(F)	0.75	☐ ☐
	Coventry or Crewe special handstamp – railway interest – on single commem...		2.00(S)		☐
	Two reverse typesettings known —				
	Top and bottom adress lines				
	1. are 96mm apart				
	2. are 92mm apart				
(2) 1980, June	2nd Print, number unknown (Small nick as described above — repaired)...		—	0.40	☐
1980, 31 MARCH	**COTSWOLD POST OFFICES (SWPR9)**	4 Views.			
SW14					
	Print 50,000..		1.25(S)	0.30	☐ ☐
	Lower Slaughter; Sherborne; Gloucester or Bibury CDS.....		3.50(C)		☐
	Filkins, Glos CDS...		4.75(C)		☐
1980, 19 MAY	**BOURNEMOUTH ROYAL MAIL AIR SERVICES (SWPR10)**	4 Views of aircraft.			
SW15					
	Print 50,000..		1.25(S)	0.30	☐ ☐
	Bournemouth or Liverpool CDS..............................		1.50(C)		☐
	Hurn, Christchurch CDS.......................................		3.50		☐

N.B. FDI(S) known with or without cachet 'Flown on the Royal Mail Air Service' etc.

			FDI	Mint
1980, 4 JULY SW16	**FOVANT BADGES** (Normal size)**(SWPR11)** 4 Views. Print 40,000 Salisbury, Wilts/6; Fovant CDS		1.25(S) 2.25-3.25(C)	0.30 ☐ ☐ ☐

N.B. FDI(S) known with or without cachet 'Carried by Scout Helicopter' etc. Card was released by one Post Office late June.

| **1980, 4 JULY**
SW17 | **FOVANT BADGES** (Jumbo size) **(SWPR11 Jumbo)**
4 Views.
Print 20,000
Salisbury, Wilts/6; Fovant CDS | 1.25(C)
2.25-3.25(C) | 0.35 ☐ ☐
☐ |

N.B. FDI(S) known with or without cachet as SW16.

1981, 28 APRIL SW18	**ROYAL MAIL SERVICES BY FERRY (SWPR12)** 2 Views, South Devon. Print 430,000 Dartmouth or Salcombe CDS	1.00(S) 2.75(C)	0.30 ☐ ☐ ☐
1981, 29 MAY SW19	**RURAL POST IN SOMERSET (SWPR13)** 6 views – 3 P.O.'s and 'Ludlow' letter boxes Print 30,000 Allerford/Minehead, Somerset, West Monkton or Thurloxton CDS	1.00(S) 3.25(C)	0.30 ☐ ☐ ☐
1981, 1 OCTOBER SW20	**SOUTH WESTERN POSTAL REGION MAP** Jumbo size **(SWPR14)** Print 30,000 Bristol CDS; Bath, Avon/2 m/c + slogan	1.25(S) 1.75-2.00(C)	0.35 ☐ ☐ ☐
	MAIL CARRIERS BUILT IN BRISTOL Set of 4. Paintings by John G. Norriss.		
1981, 21 OCTOBER SW21	**BRISTOL-BATH-LONDON MAIL COACH (SWPR15a)** Print 30,000 Bristol CDS Bath m/c + slogan	1.00(S) 1.25(C) 5.00(C)	0.25 ☐ ☐ ☐ ☐
41981, 21 OCTOBER SW22	**SS GREAT BRITAIN (SWPR15b)** Off Avonmouth c.1845 Print 30,000 Bristol/24; Avonmouth/Bristol CDS	1.00(S) 1.50-1.75(C)	0.25 ☐ ☐ ☐
1981, 21 OCTOBER SW23	**THE AVON MERCURY TRIMOBILE (SWPR15c)** Built in Keynsham, leaving P.O. with Mail c.1905. Print 30,000 Keynsham/Bristol CDS.	1.00(S) 1.75(C)	0.25 ☐ ☐ ☐
1981, 21 OCTOBER SW24	**CONCORDE 1980 (SWPR15d)** Print 30,000 Hounslow 'Heathrow Airport' etc. Special handstamp	1.00(S) 1.25(S)	0.25 ☐ ☐ ☐
SW21-24	Set of 4 as above	4.00(S)	1.00 ☐ ☐
1982, 20 APRIL SW25	**HORSE DRAWN MAIL VAN AT BROADHEMBURY POST OFFICE (SWPR16)** Print 25,000 Broadhembury/Honiton CDS	1.00(S) 4.75(C)	0.30 ☐ ☐ ☐

N.B. Most were printed on slightly rough white card. Known also on rough cream card — £1.00.

| **1982, 21 MAY**
SW26 | **ROYAL MAIL DELIVERING TO HMS AMBUSCADE (SWPR17)**
Print 25,000
Plymouth/Cornwall & W.Devon m/c + slogan | 1.00(S)
1.25(C) | 0.30 ☐ ☐
☐ |
| **1982, 23 JUNE**
SW27 | **EMPIRE AIRMAIL, 1937, SOUTHAMPTON (SWPR18)**
Painting of Flying Boats by John G. Norriss.
Print 20,000
Southampton CDS
28 JUNE '82 Southampton '45th Anniv. Flight' | 1.00(S)
1.60(C)
1.25(S) | 0.30 ☐ ☐
☐
☐ |

N.B. Most were printed on slightly rough white card. Known also on smooth off white card — 90p.

		FDI	Mint	
1983, 10 MAY SW28	**FALMOUTH PACKET 'FRANCIS FREELING' (SWPR19)** Print 16,000 Falmouth CDS	1.00(S) 1.60(C)	0.30	☐ ☐ ☐
1983, 3 AUGUST SW29	**PARCEL POST CENTENARY (SWPR20)** Features Henry Fawcett born in Salisbury. Print 16,000 Salisbury/Wilts. CDS on £1.30 definitive also issued 3 August.	1.00(S) 1.25(C) 3.00(C)(S)(F)	0.30	☐ ☐ ☐ ☐
1983, 19 OCTOBER SW30	**GWK POST OFFICE VAN AT CHELTENHAM c.1920 (SWPR21)** Painting by John Norriss. Print 16,000 Cheltenham CDS	1.00(S) 1.50(C)	0.30	☐ ☐ ☐
1984, 30 MAY SW31	**ROYAL MAIL COACH (SWPR22)** Used in the re-enactment of the 1784 run from Bristol to London. Print 25,000 Bath/Avon CDS in violet. 31 JULY '84 Bath or Bristol handstamp (Commemorative run – various known) on 16p Mail Coach commemorative	1.00(S) 1.50(C) 1.00(S)	0.35	☐ ☐ ☐ ☐
1984, 6 JUNE SW32	**NEW WEYMOUTH MURAL (SWPR23)** Third panel of the PO mural. Issued on 40th anniversary of 'D-Day'. Print 25,000 Weymouth or other 'D-Day' special handstamp Weymouth/Dorset CDS	1.00(S) 1.00(S) 1.50(C)	0.35	☐ ☐ ☐ ☐
1984, 17 AUGUST SW33	**SWPR HOT-AIR BALLOON (SWPR24)** Photograph of Hot-Air Balloon from below. Print 16,000 Known with PO cachet 'Carried in the Royal Mail Hot-Air Balloon — G-SWPR' Bristol/34 CDS or Philatelic Counter special handstamp	1.00(S) from 1.25(C)	0.35	☐ ☐ ☐
1985, 25 APRIL SW34	**BROAD GAUGE ENGINE IN BRISTOL OLD TEMPLE MEADS STATION (SWPR25)** Painting by John G. Norriss. Print 16,000 Bristol CDS	1.00(S) 1.50(C)	0.35	☐ ☐ ☐
1985, 6 JUNE SW35	**'THE CHELTENHAM FLYER' (SWPR26)** Painting by John G. Norriss Print 16,000 Cheltenham/Glos. CDS	1.00(S) 1.50(C)	0.35	☐ ☐ ☐
1985, 6 JUNE SW36	**THE 'CITY OF TRURO' LOCO. (SWPR27)** Painting by John G. Norriss. Print 16,000 Truro/Cornwall CDS.	1.00(S) 1.50(C)	0.25	☐ ☐ ☐
1985, 1 AUGUST SW37	**THE 'EVENING STAR' LOCO. (SWPR28)** Painting by John G. Norriss. Print 20,000	1.00(S)	0.25	☐ ☐
	LINKS WITH THE POST OFFICE AND THE RAF Set of 4. Paintings by John G. Norriss.			
1986, 30 SEPTEMBER SW38	**BRISTOL BRITANNIA CMK1 (SWPR29)** Print 16,000 Bristol CDS or Philatelic Counter Special handstamp	1.00(S) 1.25(C)(S)	0.25	☐ ☐ ☐
1986, 30 SEPTEMBER SW39	**DE HAVILLAND COMET 4C (SWPR30)** Print 16,000 Bristol CDS or Philatelic Counter Special handstamp	1.00(S) 1.25(C)(S)	0.25	☐ ☐ ☐
1986, 30 SEPTEMBER SW40	**DH9A AND BRISTOL F2B (SWPR31)** Print 16,000 Bristol CDS or Philatelic Counter Special handstamp	1.00(S) 1.25(C)(S)	0.25	☐ ☐ ☐
1986, 30 SEPTEMBER SW41	**C130 HERCULES MK3 & MK1 (SWPR32)** Print 16,000 Bristol CDS or Philatelic Counter Special handstamp Two special handstamps in use at Bristol 'First day of sale' and 'Final issue of SWPR Postcards'	1.00(S) 1.25(C)(S)	0.25	☐ ☐ ☐
SW38-41	Set of 4	4.00(S)	1.00	☐ ☐

SPECIAL OFFERS OF BENHAM LUXURY 'SILK' CARDS

SCO.77 BPC85(3)
Music. Set of 4
.... **£6.00**

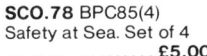

SCO.78 BPC85(4)
Safety at Sea. Set of 4
.... **£5.00**

SCO.79 BPC85(5)
350th Anniversary P.O.
Set of 4 .... **£5.00**

SCO.80 BPC85(8)
Christmas. Set of 5 .... **£6.50**

SCO.81 BPC 86(3) 60th Birthday. Set of 4 .... **£6.00**

SCO.82 ALL 5 SETS **£25.00**

(A. Buckingham) Ltd.
Westcliff House,
Folkestone, Kent
CT20 1SZ

WALES AND THE MARCHES POSTAL REGION

Cards can be obtained from:

Philatelic Counter
2-4 Hills Street
CARDIFF CF1 2ST

Philatelic Counter
2 St. John Street
CHESTER CH1 1AA

Philatelic Counter
Broad Street
HEREFORD HR1 1AA

Philatelic Counter
High Street
NEWPORT
Gwent NPT 1AZ

Philatelic Counter
St. Mary's Street
SHREWSBURY SY1 1AA

Philatelic Counter
35 The Kingsway
SWANSEA SA1 5LF

Wales and the Marches Postal Board
35 The Parade
Roath
CARDIFF CF2 3TA

			FDI	Mint	
	REGIONAL VIEWS WITH POSTAL INTEREST. Set of 8.				
1974, 7 AUGUST WM1	**CIVIC CENTRE, CARDIFF (WMPB1)** Print 8,100...		5.00(S)	1.75	☐ ☐
1974, 7 AUGUST WM2	**ST. DAVID'S CATHEDRAL, HAVERFORD WEST (WMPB2)** Print 8,100...		5.00(S)	1.75	☐ ☐
1974, 7 AUGUST WM3	**LLANIDLOES POSTBUS (WMPB3)** Print 8,100...		5.00(S)	5.00	☐ ☐
1974, 7 AUGUST WM4	**BRECON BEACONS NATIONAL PARK (WMPB4)** Print 8,100...		5.00(S)	1.75	☐ ☐
1974, 7 AUGUST WM5	**LLANGORSE LAKE (WMPB5)** Print 8,100...		5.00(S)	1.75	☐ ☐
1974, 7 AUGUST WM6	**CASWELL BAY, GOWER PENINSULA (WMPB6)** Print 8,100...		5.00(S)	1.75	☐ ☐
1974, 7 AUGUST WM7	**EASTGATE CLOCK TOWER, CHESTER (WMPB7)** Print 8,100...		5.00(S)	1.75	☐ ☐
1974, 7 AUGUST WM8	**LLEDR BRIDGE, BETS-Y-COED (WMPB8)** Print 8,100...		5.00(S)	1.75	☐ ☐
WM1-8	Set of 8 as above		39.00(S)	17.00	☐
	VIEWS WITH A LOCAL POSTBUS. Set of 6.				
1979, 10 JANUARY WM9	**LLANDRINDOD WELLS POSTBUS (WMPB9)**				
(1) 1979, 10 January	1st Print 5,000 (Guillotined from front)......................		1.00(S)	0.50	☐ ☐
(2) 1979, — January	2nd Print 10,000 (Guillotined from back)....................		2.00(S)	0.40	☐ ☐
	Llandrindod Wells/Powys CDS or m/c.............. (1) or (2)		2.25(C)		☐
1979, 10 JANUARY WM10	**LLANDOVERY POSTBUS, LLANDOVERY (WMPB10)**				
(1) 1979, 10 January	1st Print 5,000 (Guillotined from front)......................		1.00(S)	0.50	☐ ☐
(2) 1979, — January	2nd Print 10,000 (Guillotined from back)....................		2.00(S)	0.40	☐ ☐
	Llandovery/Dyfed CDS .... (1) or (2)		2.25(C)		☐
1979, 10 JANUARY WM11	**LLANIDLOES POSTBUS (WMPB11)**				
(1) 1979, 10 January	1st Print 5,000 (Guillotined from front)......................		1.00(S)	0.50	☐ ☐
(2) 1979, — January	2nd Print 10,000 (Guillotined from back)....................		2.00(C)	0.40	☐ ☐
	Llanidloes/Powys CDS .... (1) or (2)		2.25(C)		☐
1979, 10 JANUARY WM12	**RHYL POSTBUS, GROESFFORD (WMPB12)**				
(1) 1979, January	1st Print 5,000 (Guillotined from front)......................		1.00(S)	0.50	☐ ☐
(2) 1979, — January	2nd Print 10,000 (Guillotined from back)....................		2.00(S)	0.40	☐ ☐
	Clwyd/2A CDS... (1) or (2)		2.25(C)		☐
1979, 10 JANUARY WM13	**USK POSTBUS, USK (WMPB13)**				
(1) 1979, 10 January	1st Print 5,000 (Guillotined from front)......................		1.00(S)	0.50	☐ ☐
(2) 1979, — January	2nd Print 10,000 (Guillotined from back)....................		2.00(S)	0.40	☐ ☐
	Usk P.S.O./Gwent CDS .... (1) or (2)		2.25(C)		☐

			FDI	Mint

1979, 10 JANUARY — **USK POSTBUS, RAGLAN (WMPB14)**
WM14

		FDI	Mint
(1) 1979, 10 January	1st Print 5,000 (Guillotined from front).....................	1.00(S)	0.50 ☐ ☐
(2) 1979, — January	2nd Print 10,000 (Guillotined from back).................	2.00(S)	0.40 ☐ ☐
	Usk P.S.O./Gwent CDS .... (1) or (2)	2.25(C)	☐
WM9-14	Set of 6 as above. 1st Print................................	5.25(S)	2.75 ☐ ☐
WM9-14	Set of 6 as above. 2nd Print...............................	11.00(S)	2.20 ☐ ☐

N.B. As advance orders for this set were in excess of the number printed a second print was made. Both are available with the FDI cancel. Postbus cachets are known on WM9, 10, 13 and 14.

1981, 13 JULY — **AERIAL VIEW OF SHREWSBURY**
WM15 — View of Central Postal Delivery Area. **WMPB15** (not printed on card).

		FDI	Mint
(1) 1981, 13 July	1st print 5,000 ("Address" printed above the address lines)...	1.20(S)	0.80 ☐ ☐
	Shewsbury/5 CDS	2.00(C)	☐
(2) 1981, 13 July	2nd Print 12,500 (As 1st Print but without the word "Address")	1.20(S)	0.30 ☐ ☐
	Shrewsbury, Shropshire/4 CDS, m/c slogan	2.00(C)	☐

N.B. 2nd Print, with "Address" removed to provide clear space for special handstamp, was necessary to meet first day orders.

1981, 2 NOVEMBER — **THE SHREWSBURY-YORK TRAVELLING POST OFFICE**
WM16 — Loading mail onto the train. **WMPB16** (not printed on card)

	FDI	Mint
Print 22,000 Shrewsbury or York special handstamp	2.00(S)	0.50 ☐ ☐
Shrewsbury-York or York-Shrewsbury TPO CDS.............	2.00(C)	☐
Shrewsbury, Shropshire/4 or York CDS.....................	2.25(C)	☐

1981, 2 NOVEMBER — **THE SHREWSBURY-YORK TRAVELLING POST OFFICE**
WM17 — Sorting mail inside the train. **WMPB17** (not printed on card)

	FDI	Mint
Print 22,000 Shrewsbury or York special Handstamp.	2.00(S)	0.50 ☐ ☐
Shrewsbury-York or York-Shrewsbury TPO CDS.............	2.00(C)	☐
Shrewsbury, Shropshire/4 or York CDS.....................	2.25(C)	☐

WM16 and 17 were sold at Shrewsbury from 26 October — pair CDS £10.00.

1982, 21 JANUARY — **HEREFORD HEAD POST OFFICE CENTENARY** (Local)
WM18 — Victorian photo of Broad Street PO (Giant size)

		FDI	Mint
(1) 1982, 21 January	1st Print 3,000....................................	2.50(S)	1.30 ☐ ☐
(2) 1982, 21 January	2nd Print 2,500. Reverse 'First Reprint'.....................	1.60(S)	1.20 ☐ ☐
(3) 1982, February	3rd print 5,000. Reverse 'Second Reprint'	1.20(S)	0.60 ☐ ☐

N.B. The price in the FDI column refers to cards cancelled on the 15 February with a Special Centenary Handstamp (the reason for the card issue). Cards cancelled 21 January — £20.00 each.

1982, 4 MAY — **SWANSEA PHILATELIC COUNTER** (Local)
Five views — counter, Kingsway and four local views
WM19

	FDI	Mint
Print 12,000 Swansea CDS	2.20(C)	0.30 ☐ ☐

Two reverse typesettings known —
'T' in 'The Guildhall'
   1. under 'w' in 'Abertawe'
   2. under 'aw' in 'Abertawe'

HISTORIC STAGE COACH ROUTE 1782 (Local)
Set of 5 in red wallet. (Giant size).

1982, 1 JULY — **ROAD FROM BRISTOL TO WESTCHESTER (NO. 1)**
WM20

	FDI	Mint
Print 5,000 'The Hereford Times' or Hereford CDS...........	1.00(S)	0.40 ☐ ☐

1982, 1 JULY — **ROAD FROM CHEPSTOW TO HEREFORD (NO. 2)**
WM21

	FDI	Mint
Print 5,000..	1.00(S)(C)	0.40 ☐ ☐
Bristol/34 CDS..	1.25(C)	☐

1982, 1 JULY — **ROAD FROM HEREFORD TO LUDLOW (NO. 3)**
WM22

	FDI	Mint
Print 5,000...	1.00(S)	0.40 ☐ ☐
Ludlow/Salop CDS...	1.25(C)	☐

1982, 1 JULY — **ROAD FROM LUDLOW TO SHREWSBURY (NO. 4)**
WM23

	FDI	Mint
Print 5,000...	1.00(S)	0.40 ☐ ☐
Shropshire & /Mid. Wales CDS	1.25(C)	☐

Date / No.	Description	FDI	Mint		
1982, 1 JULY WM24	**ROAD FROM SHREWSBURY TO CHESTER (NO. 5)** Print 5,000. Chester CDS.	1.00(S) 1.25(C)	0.40	☐	☐
WM20-24	Set of 5 as above issued in red wallet	5.00(S)	2.00	☐	☐

N.B. An additional print of 1,500 were released with "2nd S.A.S. Regiment Dependants Appeal Fund" overprinted on the wallet, to raise money for this fund. Pack – £3.00.

1982, 17 NOVEMBER WM25	**75th ANNIVERSARY OF FORMER HPO BUILDING, NEWPORT, GWENT** (Local) Print 1,050 Newport, Gwent 'FDI'. Only 60 FDI cards are believed to exist.	35.00(F)	2.20	☐	☐

CASTLES IN WALES. Set of 6 in wallet.

1983, 27 JUNE WM26	**CASTLE COCH, CARDIFF (WMPB18)** Print 15,000 Cardiff/1 CDS or Philatelic Counter handstamp.	1.00(S) 1.50(C)(S)	0.30	☐	☐
1983, 27 JUNE WM27	**PEMBROKE CASTLE (WMPB19)** Print 15,000 Cardiff CDS; Pembroke Dock, Dyfed CDS	1.00(S) 1.50(C)	0.30	☐	☐
1983, 27 JUNE WM28	**RHUDDLAN CASTLE (WMPB20)** Print 15,000 Cardiff CDS; Rhuddlan, Rhyl/Clwyd CDS	1.00(S) 1.50(C)	0.30	☐	☐
1983, 27 JUNE WM29	**RAGLAN CASTLE (WMPB21)** Print 15,000 Cardiff CDS, Raglan/Gwent CDS	1.00(S) 1.50(C)	0.30	☐	☐
1983, 27 JUNE WM30	**BEAUMARIS CASTLE (WMPB22)** Print 15,000 Cardiff CDS; Beaumaris/Gwynedd CDS	1.00(S) 1.50(C)	0.30	☐	☐
1983, 27 JUNE WM31	**POWIS CASTLE (WMPB23)** Print 15,000 Cardiff CDS; Welshpool/Powys CDS	1.00(S) 1.50(C)	0.30	☐	☐
WM26-31	Set of 6 as above in red wallet	6.00(S)	1.75	☐	☐

N.B. On 22 January 1985 HP Bulmer Ltd/6000 Association issued a card (Print 10,000) featuring a painting of the locomotive 'King George V, by Cuneo which was also sold at Shrewsbury HPO – 50p (FDI £1.00).

REGIONAL MOBILE EXHIBTION UNIT
Set of 4.

1985, 4 MARCH WM32	**UNIT AT LLANGOLLEN INTERNATIONAL EISTEDDFOD (WMPB24)** Print 13,000 Cardiff CDS or Philatelic Counter special handstamp	1.00(S) 1.25(C)(S)	0.30	☐	☐
1985, 4 MARCH WM33	**UNIT AT ROYAL WELSH SHOW-BUILTH WELLS (WMPB25)** Print 13,000 Cardiff CDS or Philatelic Counter special handstamp	1.00(S) 1.25(C)(S)	0.30	☐	☐
1985, 4 MARCH WM34	**UNIT AT NATIONAL EISTEDDFORD-LAMPETER (WMPB26)** Print 13,000 Cardiff CDS or Philatelic Counter special handstamp	1.00(S) 1.25(C)(S)	0.30	☐	☐
1985, 4 MARCH WM35	**P.O. DISPLAY AT SHREWSBURY FLOWER SHOW (WMPB27)** Print 13,000 Cardiff or Shrewsbury CDS; Philatelic Counter special handstamp from	1.00(S) 1.25(C)(S)	0.30	☐	☐
WM32-35	Set of 4 as above	4.00(S)	1.20	☐	☐

PROMOTIONAL AND POSTCODE CARDS

1979, — JANUARY WMP1	**CWMBRAN NP44 POSTCODE NOTIFICATION** Relief panel in Gwent Square **(NP/PC/79)** Official Paid. Grey card. Print 150,000	—	1.60	☐	
1979, — JANUARY WMP2	**PONTYPOOL NP4 POSTCODE NOTIFICATION** Llandegfedd Reservoir **(NP/PC/79)** Official Paid. Blue card. Print 20,000.	—	3.20	☐	

 WM1

 WM3

 WM7

 WM9

 WM11

 WM13

 WM15

 WM16

 WM17

 WM18

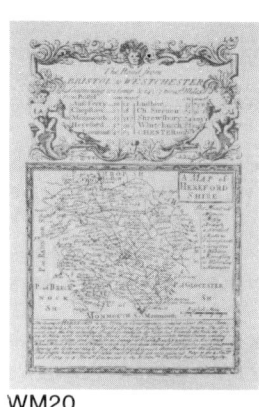 WM20

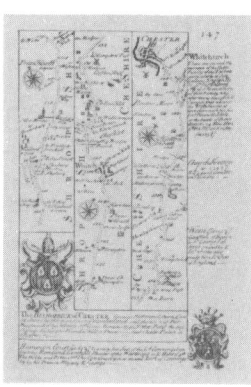 WM24

 WM25

 WM28

 WM33

SCOTTISH POSTAL REGION

Cards can be obtained from:

Philatelic Counter
65 Sandgate
AYR KA7 1AA

Philatelic Counter
2 Waterloo Place
EDINBURGH EH1 1AA

Philatelic Counter
George Square
GLASGOW G2 1AA

Philatelic Counter
14-16 Queensgate
INVERNESS IV1 1AA

Scottish Postal Board
West Port House
102 West Port
EDINBURGH EH3 9HS

			FDI	Mint		

THE POSTBUS IN SCOTLAND. 1st Series.
Set of 5 with information folder.

1979, 28 NOVEMBER — **KELSO-STICHILL POSTBUS (SPB1)**
S1
Service No. 42
Print 10,000 .... 1.00(S)   0.70 ☐ ☐
Kelso CDS; Stichill/Kelso CDS .... 3.00(C)   ☐

1979, 28 NOVEMBER — **KILLIN-CALLANDER POSTBUS (SPB2)**
S2
Service No. 68
Print 10,000 .... 1.00(S)   0.70 ☐ ☐
Callander CDS; Stirling/2 CDS; Stirling 'FDI' .... 3.00(C)(F)   ☐

1979, 28 NOVEMBER — **KIRKCUDBRIGHT-BORGUE POSTBUS (SPB3)**
S3
Service No. 87
Print 10,000 .... 1.00(S)   0.70 ☐ ☐
Kirkcudbright CDS; Borgue/Kirkcudbright CDS .... 3.00(C)   ☐

1979, 28 NOVEMBER — **INVERARAY-DAMALLY POSTBUS (SPB4)**
S4
Service No. 100
Print 10,000 .... 100(S)   0.70 ☐ ☐
Inveraray/Argyll CDS; Dalmally/Argyll CDS .... 3.00(C)   ☐

1979, 28 NOVEMBER — **BRODICK-SHANNOCHIE POSTBUS (SPB5)**
S5
Service No. 104
Print 10,000 .... 1.00(S)   0.70 ☐ ☐
Brodick/Isle-of-Arran CDS................................. 3.00(C)   ☐

S1-5   Set of 5 as above in plastic pack .... 4.75(S)   3.50 ☐ ☐

N.B. Sets were issued by Scottish Postal Board rubber stamped 'SPECIMEN' in violet, reverse — £28.00.

THE POSTBUS IN SCOTLAND. 2nd Series.
Set of 5 with information folder.

1980, 16 JULY — **BETTYHILL-KINBRACE POSTBUS (SPB6)**
S6
Service No. 21
Print 10,000 .... 1.00(S)   0.50 ☐ ☐
Bettyhill CDS .... 3.00(C)   ☐

1980, 16 JULY — **GROTAIG-DRUMNADROCHIT POSTBUS (SPB7)**
S7
Service No. 53
Print 10,000 .... 1.00(S)   0.50 ☐ ☐

1980, 16 JULY — **ARNISDALE-KYLE OF LOCHALSH POSTBUS (SPB8)**
S8
Service No. 59
Print 10,000 .... 1.00(S)   0.50 ☐ ☐

1980, 16 JULY — **COLONSAY P.O.-KILORAN POSTBUS (SPB9)**
S9
Service No. 78
Print 10,000 .... 1.00(S)   0.50 ☐ ☐

1980, 16 JULY — **BALLATER-LINN OF DEE POSTBUS (SPB10)**
S10
Service No. 13
Print 10,000 .... 1.00(S)   0.50 ☐ ☐

S6-10 Set of 5 as above in plastic pack .... 4.75(S)   2.50 ☐ ☐

N.B. Sets were issued by Scottish Postal Board rubber stamped 'SPECIMEN' in violet, reverse — £35.00.

ST. ANDREW'S AMBULANCE ASSOCIATION CENTENARY
Set of 4 with paper information folder.

1982, 23 JUNE — **GLASGOW FIRST AID TEAM IN COMPETITION (SPB11)**
S11
Print 10,000 .... 1.20(S)   0.30 ☐ ☐
Glasgow CDS; Philatelic Counter handstamp....... 1.50(C)(S)   ☐

			FDI	Mint	
1982, 23 JUNE S12	**POST OFFICE MEMBERS OF ST. ANDREW'S AMBULANCE CORPS (SPB12)** Print 10,000 Glasgow CDS; Philatelic Counter handstamp		1.20(S) 1.50(C)(S)	0.30	☐ ☐ ☐
1982, 23 JUNE S13	**DELIVERY OF MAIL TO HEADQUARTERS OF ST. ANDREW'S AMBULANCE ASSOCIATION (SPB13)** Print 10,000 Glasgow CDS; Philatelic Counter handstamp		1.20(S) 1.50(C)(S)	0.30	☐ ☐ ☐
1982, 23 JUNE S14	**ROYAL MAIL POSTBUS MEETS MOBILE FIRST AID POST (SPB14)** Print 10,000 Glasgow CDS; Philatelic Counter handstamp		1.20(S) 1.50(C)(S)	0.30	☐ ☐ ☐
S11-14	Set of 4 as above with paper information folder		4.50(S)	1.00	☐ ☐
	CENTENARY OF THE CROFTERS HOLDINGS (SCOTLAND) ACT 1886 Set of 6 with descriptive folder in plastic pack. Based on paintings by Edinburgh artist Archie MacAlister. Inscriptions English/Gaelic.				
1986, 2 JUNE S15	**ISLAND LOBSTERMAN (SPOB15)** Print 25,000 Inverness Phil. Counter special handstamp 15 JUNE '86 Inverness or Edinburgh special handstamp 'Crofters Act 1886-1986'		1.00(S) 1.00(S)	0.25	☐ ☐ ☐
1986, 2 JUNE S16	**LANDING ISLAND SHEEP (SPOB16)** Print 25,000 Inversness Phil. Counter special handstamp 15 JUNE '86 Inverness or Edinburgh special handstamp 'Crofters Act 1886-1986'		1.00(S) 1.00(S)	0.25	☐ ☐ ☐
1986, 2 JUNE S17	**COMMUNICATIONS (SPOB17)** Print 25,000 Inverness Phil. Counter special handstamp 15 JUNE '86 Inverness or Edinburgh special handstamp 'Crofters Act 1886-1986'		1.00(S) 1.00(S)	0.25	☐ ☐ ☐
1986, 2 JUNE S18	**MORNING IN WESTER ROSS (SPOB18)** Print 25,000 Inverness Phil. Counter special handstamp 15 JUNE '86 Inverness or Edinburgh special handstamp 'Crofters Act 1886-1986'		1.00(S) 1.00(S)	0.25	☐ ☐ ☐
1986, 2 JUNE S19	**HEBRIDEAN MALT (SPOB19)** Print 25,000 Inverness Phil. Counter special handstamp 15 JUNE '86 Inverness or Edinburgh special handstamp 'Crofters Act 1886-1986'		1.00(S) 1.00(S)	0.25	☐ ☐ ☐
1986, 2 JUNE S20	**WEATHER IN CAITHNESS (SPOB20)** Print 25,000 Inverness Phil. Counter special handstamp 15 JUNE '86 Inverness or Edinburgh special handstamp 'Crofters Act 1886-1986'		1.00(S) 1.00(S)	0.25	☐ ☐ ☐
S15-20	Set of 6 as above in plastic pack		5.25(S)	150	☐ ☐
	10,000 packs were issued. Remainder of print were issued as single cards.				

AIRLETTERS

We have decided this year to leave out the Air Letter Section. For those of you who collect Air Letters and want further information may we recommend that you contact Bernard Townsend, Bredon Hill Stamps, PO Box 12, Evesham, Worcestershire. Bernard has the largest stock of GB Air Letters in the country and would, I am sure, be able to provide you with a good reference list and help you with your hobby.

NORTHERN IRELAND POSTAL REGION

Cards can be obtained from:

Philatelic Counter
51-63 Wellington Street
BALLYMENA
Co. Antrim BT43 6AA

Philatelic Counter
25 Castle Street
BELFAST
BT1 1BB

N. Ireland Postal Board
14 Queen Street
BELFAST BT1 6ER

Philatelic Counter
3 Custom House Street
LONDONDERRY
BT48 6AA

Philatelic Counter
William Street BO
PORTADOWN, Craigavon
Co. Armagh BT62 1MX

		FDI	Mint		
1986, 2 JANUARY	**CITY OF BELFAST YOUTH ORCHESTRA (NIPB1)**				
	A section of the youth orchestra outside Castle Place Post Office, Belfast				
NI1	Print 12,000	1.00(S)	0.25	☐	☐
	Belfast/1, Londonderry/12 or other CDS	1.50(C)		☐	
	Belfast or other N.I. Phil Counter special handstamp	1.25(S)		☐	
1986, 2 JANUARY	**LISBANE POST OFFICE (NIPB2)**				
	Photo of Lisbane PO. County Down, over 200 years old.				
NI2	Print 12,000	1.00(S)	0.25	☐	☐
	Portadown BO; Belfast/1 or other CDS	1.50(C)		☐	
	Belfast or other N.I. Phil. Counter special handstamp	1.25(S)		☐	
	Belfast FDI (applied incorrectly as no new commem. or definitive stamps were issued 2 Jan.)	3.00(F)		☐	

NATIONAL POSTAL MUSEUM

Cards can be obtained from:
The National Postal Museum
King Edward Street
LONDON EC1A 1LP

Many of the Museum's cards are also obtainable from the Philatelic Bureau, Edinburgh and some Philatelic Counters

The Museum is open from 10 a.m.'— 4.30 p.m. Monday to Thursday and 10 a.m. — 4.00 p.m. Fridays, admission free. Closed weekends, Bank and Public Holidays.

The Reginald M. Phillips collection of 19th century British Postage Stamps is one of the major collections housed at the museum.

(S) cancels are the Museum's own 'Maltese Cross' special handstamp or its special exhibition handstamps which have been in use for limited periods only since 1981.

Museum and Historic Series Cards

Series 1 to 5 Museum series 1st prints were issued in envelopes with straight flaps. 2nd print envelopes had pointed flaps. 3rd print envelopes had wider straight flaps and larger reference numbers in stamp box.

		FDI	Mint	
1969, NOVEMBER PM1	**EARLY POSTAL PERSONALITIES (Series 1)** Set of 6 cards in printed envelope.			
	1/1 Jacob Perkins — 1/4 William Wyon			
	1/2 Charles Heath — 1/5 Henry Cole			
	1/3 Rowland Hill — 1/6 Henry Corbould			
(1) 1969, November	1st Print 20,000 (Reference number lower left on reverse of cards)	—	2.50	☐
(2) 1979, January	2nd Print 20,000 (No reference number)	—	1.50	☐
1969, NOVEMBER PM2	**DEVELOPMENT OF THE PENNY BLACK (Series 2)** Set of 6 cards in printed envelope.			
	2/1 Wyon City Medal — 2/4 'Penny Black'			
	2/2 H. Corbould's Drawings — 2/5 Water Colour Sketch			
	2/3 2d. Specimen 1840 — 2/6 2d. 'Blue'			
(1) 1969, November	1st Print 20,000 (Reference number lower left on reverse of cards)	—	28.50	☐
(2) 1978, 4 May	2nd Print 20,000 (No reference number)	50.00(S)	2.00	☐ ☐
(3) 1981, 2 November	3rd Print (as 2nd Print but thicker card)	5.50(S)	1.50	☐ ☐
1969, NOVEMBER PM3	**MULREADY (Series 3)** Set of 6 cards in printed envelope.			
	3/1 W. Mulready — 3/4 Temperance Envelope			
	3/2 Mulready Envelope — 3/5 Propaganda Envelope			
	3/3 Mulready Caricature — 3/6 'Penny Pink'			
(1) 1969, November	1st Print 20,000 (Reference number lower left on reverse of cards)	—	2.50	☐
(2) 1978, October	2nd Print 20,000 (No reference number)	—	1.50	☐
1969, NOVEMBER PM4	**DE LA RUE (Series 4)** Set of 6 cards in printed envelope.			
	4/1 1/- Design — 4/4 6d. Die Proof			
	4/2 Thomas De la Rue — 4/5 1/- Die Proof			
	4/3 J.F. Joubert — 4/6 9d. Die Proofs			
(1) 1969, November	1st Print 20,000 (Reference number lower left on reverse of cards)	—	2.00	☐
(2) 1979, March	2nd Print 20,000 (No reference number)	—	1.50	☐
1969, NOVEMBER PM5	**QUEEN VICTORIA JUBILEE ESSAYS (Series 5)** Set of 6 cards in printed envelope.			
	5/1 De la Rue Essays — 5/4 W. Adams's Scheme			
	5/2 1½d. Artist's Drawing — 5/5 1887 Jubilee Issue			
	5/3 Colour Essays — 5/6 High Values 1883			
(1) 1969, November	1st Print 20,000 (Reference number lower left on reverse of cards)	—	13.00	☐
(2) 1978, 4 May	2nd Print 20,000 (No reference number)	50.00(S)	2.00	☐ ☐
(3) 1981, 2 November	3rd Print (as 2nd Print but thicker card)	5.50(S)	1.50	☐ ☐
1980, 6 MAY PM6	**EDWARD VII ESSAYS (Series 6)** Set of 6 cards in printed envelope.			
	6/1 Preliminary Essays — 6/4 7d. Designs			
	6/2 The Fuchs Portrait — 6/5 2d. Tyrian Plum			
	6/3 Approved 1d. Design — 6/6 6d. and ½d. Stamps			
	Print 30,000	6.00(S)	1.50	☐ ☐

		FDI	Mint

1980, 6 MAY
PM7
GEORGE V DEFINITIVE STAMP ESSAYS (Series 7)
Set of 6 cards in printed envelope.
- 7/1 Unofficial Essays
- 7/2 Royal Mint Designs
- 7/3 Downey Head Issue
- 7/4 1912 Designs
- 7/5 Mackennal Head
- 7/6 Colour Essays

Print 30,000 .... 6.00(S) 1.50 ☐ ☐

1980, 6 MAY
PM8
GEORGE V COMMEMORATIVE STAMP ESSAYS (Series 8)
Set of 6 cards in printed envelope.
- 8/1 1924/5 Wembley
- 8/2 1929 PUC
- 8/3 1929 £1 PUC
- 8/4 £1 PUC Colour Trials
- 8/5 1935 Silver Jubilee
- 8/6 KGV Memorial Essays

Print 30,000 .... 6.00(S) 1.50 ☐ ☐

1982, 1 NOVEMBER
PM9
KING EDWARD VIII ESSAYS (Series 9)
Set of 4 cards in printed envelope.
- 9.1 Coronation Essays
- 9.2 Kings Head Essays
- 9.3 Definitive Essays
- 9.4 1936 Issue Essays

Print 30,000 .... 5.00(S) 2.50 ☐ ☐

1984, 31 JULY
PM10
DEVELOPMENT OF THE MAIL COACH (Series H1)
Set of 5 cards in printed envelope.
- H1/1 Dover Coach c.1787
- H1/2 Exeter Coach c.1797
- H1/3 Holyhead and London Coach c.1815
- H1/4 Norwich and London Coach c.1830
- H1/5 Edinburgh and London Coach c.1836

Print 20,000 .... 5.25(S) 2.00 ☐ ☐

1985, 30 JULY
PM11
POST OFFICE UNIFORMS (Series H2)
Set of 5 cards in printed envelope.
- H2/1 Mounted Postboy c.1780
- H2/2 PO Bellman c.1820
- H2/3 London Letter Carrier c.1855
- H2/4 Postman and Penfold pillar box c.1880
- H2/5 Postman emptying rural letterbox c.1936

Print 16,400 .... 5.25(S) 2.00 ☐ ☐

1986, 14 JANUARY
PM12
POST OFFICE VANS (Series H3)
Set of 4 cards in printed envelope.
- H3/1 1933 Morris Minor
- H3/2 1936 Morris 8
- H3/3 1947 Morris 5cwt
- H3/4 1956 Morris Minor 5cwt

Print 10,500 .... 4.00(S) 1.50 ☐ ☐

Publicity Cards

1971, — —
PC1
THE PENNY BLACK
Depicts a Penny Black with corner letters "P" and "M"
Print number unknown .... — 30.00 ☐

1978, 4 MAY
PC2
THE PENNY BLACK
Depicts a Penny Black with corner letters "N" and "J" and revised wording above stamp.

(1) 1978, 4 May 1st Print 8,000 (Thin card, green appearance) .... 10.00(S) 1.50 ☐ ☐

N.B. Originally intended to be placed on sale 8 May.
Cancelled 6 May — National Stamp Day handstamp — £5.
Cancelled 8 May — NPM 'Maltese Cross' handstamp — £3.

(2) 1978, 22 June 2nd Print 20,000 (Thin card, pink appearance)............. 2.25(S) 0.60 ☐ ☐
(3) 1981, May 3rd Print 10,000 (Thick card, brown appearance) .... — 0.40 ☐

1982, 1 MARCH
PC3
MACHIN HEAD (RED) (A/3)
Print 25,000 .... 1.25(S) 0.30 ☐ ☐

1983, 30 MARCH
PC4
MACHIN HEAD (BLUE) (A/4)
Print 21,000 .... 1.25(S) 0.30 ☐ ☐

1984, 1 MAY
PC5
ROYAL MAIL POSTAGE LABEL 16p (A/5)
Print 17,500 .... 2.25(S) 4.50 ☐ ☐

1984, 28 AUGUST
PC6
MACHIN HEAD (GREEN) (A/6)
Print 27,900... 1.00(S) 0.30 ☐ ☐

PM1/1

PM2/4

PM3/2

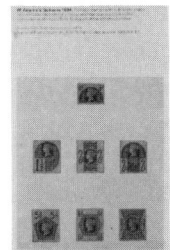
PM5/4

PM7/3

PM9/3

PC3

PC5

PE3

PE4

PE7

PE9

PE12

PE14

PE15

PE18

PE21

Exhibition and Special Series Cards

1979, 22 AUGUST   **SIR ROWLAND HILL**
PE1
Set of 5 cards in printed envelope.   FDI   Mint
    1 Portrait   2 Reform Pamphlet
    3 Post Office Journal   4 Casket
    5 Sir Rowland Hill Statue, London EC
Print 30,000 ....   7.50(S)   1.50 ☐ ☐

    N.B.   This issue coincided with the Post Office Rowland Hill stamps and cards are known wth special handstamp of Kidderminster, Bruce Castle Museum and London Chief Office (Rowland Hill statue) and others. Prices for each card from £2.00.

1981, 29 JANUARY   **POST OFFICE RIFLES (SS/1)**
PE2
From a painting by Terence Cuneo
Print 7,500 approx. ....   6.00(S)   9.00 ☐ ☐

1981, 6 FEBRUARY   **VALENTINE TELEGRAM (SS/2)**
PE3
Showing an impression of an 18th Century Post Office
Print 6,500 ....   7.50(S)   9.00 ☐ ☐

1981, 6 MAY   **MACHIN HEAD (Black) (SS/3)**
PE4
By Arnold Machin
Print 15,000 approx. ....   5.25(S)   2.50 ☐ ☐
Issued for National Stamp Day.

1981, 22 JULY   **PRINCE OF WALES MARRIAGE, PO NOTICE (SS/4)**
PE5
Shows notice isued in March 1863
Print 11,000 ....   4.25(S)   3.00 ☐ ☐

    N.B.   Issued on first day of Royal Wedding stamps – with various special handstamps £3.50 each.

1981, 1 SEPTEMBER   **AIR MAIL LETTER BOX (SS/6)**
PE6
Print 18,000 ....   2.50(S)   1.00 ☐ ☐
Sold at the Museum from this date but officially pre-released 31 August — Bedford 'Anniv. Aerial Post' handstamp — £2.25.

1981, 30 SEPTEMBER   **ANNIVERSARY OF THE FIRST U.K. AERIAL POST (SS/5)**
PE7
Print 25,000 ....   2.00(S)   0.75 ☐ ☐
Sold at the Museum from this date but officially pre-released 31 August — Bedford 'Anniv. Aerial Post' handstamp – £2.25.
9 Sept. and 11 Sept. BFPS handstamp — £1.75.

1982, 21 APRIL   **THE POST OFFICE AT WAR (Part 1) (SS/7)**
PE8
Print 16,000 ....   1.25(S)   0.50 ☐ ☐
Forces PO/965; Instanbul (Turkey) CDS etc. .... from   1.75(C)   ☐

1982, 6 MAY   **EDMUND DULAC ESSAY (SS/8)**
PE9
Print 20,000 ....   1.25(S)   0.40 ☐ ☐
London EC1 'NPM ARMY BAG' or 'NSD Nat. Postal Museum' Special handstamp ....   1.30(S)   ☐
London WC2 'NSD Covent Garden' Special handstamp .....   1.40(S)   ☐

    N.B.   Issued on National Stamp Day. With French stamp FDI Paris special handstamp — £2.50.
With various Philex-France postmarks 9-22 June '82 — from £3.00.
With additional Paris 'Museum Galerie Theodore Champion' special handstamp 24 Nov. '84 — £3.50.

1982, 7 JUNE   **MARITIME ENGLAND (SS/9)**
PE10
Print 15,000 ....   1.25(S)   0.40 ☐ ☐
Harwich CDS; Hellevoetslus (Netherlands) CDS etc. ..... from   2.25(C)   ☐

1982, 28 JUNE   **BLUE TIT ON WALL LETTER BOX (RS/1)**
PE11
Issued jointly with RSPB.
Print 12,000 ....   2.00(S)   1.50 ☐ ☐
Bedford; Birmingham; Coventry CDS etc. ....   2.50(C)   ☐
5 JULY '82 (to 8 JULY) Kenilworth 'Royal Show' handstamp...   2.00(S)   ☐

1982, 22 JULY   **THE POST OFFICE AT WAR (Part II) (SS/10)**
PE12
Print 22,500 ....   1.25(S)   0.40 ☐ ☐
BFPS 8282 Centenary special handstamp, Forces PO 10 CDS, etc. ....   1.50(S)(C)   ☐

1982, 8 SEPTEMBER   **INFORMATION TECHNOLOGY EXHIBITION (SS/12)**
PE13
Print 15,500 ....   1.25(S)   0.50 ☐ ☐

    N.B.   Issued on First day of Technology stamps – with various special handstamps — £1.50 each.

		FDI	Mint	

1982, 6 OCTOBER — **THE CENTENARY OF THE £5 ORANGE (SS/11)**
PE14
- Print 16,000 .... 1.25(S) 0.50 ☐ ☐
- Wembley 'BPE £5 1882-1982' etc. .... 1.75(S) ☐
- Wembley handstamp as above + BPE Miniature Sheet affixed and tied with cachet .... 5.00(S) ☐

1983, 6 JANUARY — **THE 1862 EXHIBITION AT SOUTH KENSINGTON (SS/13)**
PE15
- Print 14,300 .... 1.00(S) 0.40 ☐ ☐
- London SW 'International Boat Show' or other handstamp... 1.00(S) ☐
- London EC/31; Wembley/Middx. or other CDS .... 1.25(C) ☐

1983, 18 APRIL — **ROYAL MINT EXHIBITION (SS/14)**
PE16
- Print 15,000 .... 1.00(S) 0.50 ☐ ☐
- London EC 'National coin week NPM' etc. .... 1.00(S) ☐
- London EC/31 CDS or Pontyclun CDS .... 1.50(C) ☐

1983, 6 MAY — **SEAHORSE 5/- (SS/15)**
PE17
- Print 14,200 .... 1.00(S) 0.40 ☐ ☐
- London EC1 'National stamp day' etc. .... 1.00(S) ☐

1983, 6 JULY — **POST OFFICE AT WAR (Part III) (SS/16)**
PE18
- Print 15,000 .... 1.00(S) 0.40 ☐ ☐
- 'FDI' London EC. 'Forces P.O. – 10' CDS or special handstamp on army commemorative (FD) .... 1.50(C)(S)(F) ☐

1983, 24 AUGUST — **ROSES – 6d. BOTANICAL CONGRESS (SS/17)**
Reproduction of Inter. Botanical Congress commemorative of 1964 (Roses – A Thematic Display exhibition).
PE19
- Print 14,000 .... 1.00(S) 0.40 ☐ ☐
- London EC/31 CDS or 'FDI' on Gardens commemorative.... 1.20(C)(F) ☐
- Brentford; Oxford etc. special handstamp on commemorative 1.25(S) ☐

1983, 10 OCTOBER — **WYON MEDAL OF 1837 (SS/19)**
Wyon medal, 'VR' one penny black and two penny blue stamps (RM Phillips Collection – new presentation).
PE20
- Print 15,000 .... 1.00(S) 0.40 ☐ ☐
- London EC CDS or m/c slogan .... 1.25(C) ☐
- Alford, Lincs or other special handstamp .... from 1.25(S) ☐

1983, 26 OCTOBER — **ESSAYS FROM 1958 COUNTRY STAMP ISSUE (SS/18)**
Six unadopted essays (25th Anniversary of Country Stamps exhibition).
PE21
- Print 12,000 .... 1.25(S) 0.40 ☐ ☐
- Edinburgh; Belfast or Cardiff CDS .... 1.50(C) ☐
- Guernsey; Jersey or I.O.M. CDS .... 1.75(C) ☐

1984, 5 JANUARY — **INSTONE AIRLINE POSTER c.1921 (SS/20)**
An Air Parcel poster (British Airmail Services exhibition).
PE22
- Print 12,000 .... 1.00(S) 0.40 ☐ ☐
- London EC CDS or Heathrow Airport, Hounslow special handstamp .... 1.25(C)(S) ☐
- Paris or Brussels CDS .... 2.50(C) ☐

1984, 17 JANUARY — **HERALDRY – 5/- and 10/- KG VI HIGH VALUES (SS/21)**
Reproductions of 1939 stamps (Heraldry exhibition).
PE23
- Print 11,000 .... 1.00(S) 0.40 ☐ ☐
- London EC4 'College of Arms' or other special handstamp on Heraldry commemorative .... 1.25(S) ☐
- London EC CDS; London on other 'FDI' on commemorative from 1.25(C)(F) ☐

1984, 6 MARCH — **CAMBRIDGE SHOWGROUND 1894 (SS/22)**
PE24
- Print 11,000 .... 1.00(S) 0.40 ☐ ☐
- Cambridge CDS, 'FDI' or Philatelic Counter spec. handstamp on cattle commemorative .... 1.30(C)(S)(F) ☐
- Edinburgh 'Highland Cattle' or other spec. handstamp ...... 1.25(S) ☐

1984, 8 MAY — **BRITISH PRINTERS – SIX STAMPS (SS/23)**
Examples of six stamps of British Printers 1840-1980. Issued National Stamp Day (British Stamp Printers exhibition).
PE25
- Print 10,000 .... 1.00(S) 0.40 ☐ ☐
- London EC/31 or London I.S. M.L.O. CDS .... 1.25(C) ☐
- London 'National Stamp Day' or other spec. handstamp ..... 1.25(S) ☐

Date / Ref	Title / Description	FDI	Mint		
1984, 5 JUNE PE26	**UNIVERSAL POSTAL UNION (SS/24)** Print 13,000 .... London SW 'FDI' pictorial or other CDS on 31p London Summit commemorative... Berne or Hamburg handstamp .... 19 JUNE '84 Hamburg 'XIX Congress UPU'	1.00(S) 1.25(C) 2.50(S) 3.00(S)	0.40	☐	☐ ☐ ☐ ☐
1984, 26 JUNE PE27	**NAVIGATION AND ASTRONOMY (SS/25)** Print 11,000 .... London; Louth; Cambridge etc. 'FDI' on commemorative; Greenwich or other 'Meridian Cent' Special handstamp..... London EC or IS CDS or m/c	1.00(S) 1.25(S)(F) 1.50(C)	0.40	☐	☐ ☐ ☐
1984, 31 JULY PE28	**MAGGS 'OLD COACHING LINES' (SS/26)** Painting reproduction (Carriage of mail by coach exhibition). Print 15,000 .... Bath Special 'Mail Coach' or other special handstamp on commemorative.. Edinburgh/19 or other CDS on commemorative .... 2 AUG. '84 Museum 'Anniv. of the Mail Coach Service'.......	1.00(S) 1.25(S) 1.50(C) 1.00(S)	0.40	☐	☐ ☐ ☐ ☐
N.B.	Also exists as 1983 Post Office Christmas Card — £10.00.				
1984, 15 OCTOBER PE29	**1/- EMBOSSED 1847 and 1/- DEFINITIVE 1856 (SS/27)** (RM Phillips Collection – new presentation). Print 15,000 .... London EC/31 or I.S. M.L.O./72 CDS	1.00(S) 1.25(C)	0.40	☐	☐ ☐
1984, 6 NOVEMBER PE30	**POST OFFICE NOTE 5/- (SS/28)** PO Postal Order c.1874 (Exhibition of Postal Orders). Print 15,000 .... Gwent CDS or m/c...	1.00(S) 1.50(C)	0.40	☐	☐ ☐
1985, 8 JANUARY PE31	**BICENTENARY OF 'THE TIMES' (SS/29)** (Newspapers and the Post Office exhibition). Print 15,000 .... London pictorial 'FDI' on booklet se-tenant definitives .... London EC 'FDI' or m/c slogan 'The Times' etc..............	1.00(S) 1.50(S) 1.50(C)	0.40	☐	☐ ☐ ☐
1985, 22 JANUARY PE32	**GREAT WESTERN POSTER c.1904 (SS/30)** With '07 GW TPO postmark superimposed. Print 15,000 .... London, Penzance etc. special handstamps on 'Famous Trains' commemoratives... Penzance or GW TPO CDS on Trains Commemoratives	1.00(S) 1.25(S) 1.50(C)	0.40	☐	☐ ☐ ☐
1985, 2 MAY PE33	**MAP OF THE LEVANT AREA IN 1900 (SS/31A)** (British Overprinted Stamps 1885-1966 exhibition). Print 15,000 .... London EC or IS CDS or m/c .... from	1.00(S) 1.30(C)	0.35	☐	☐ ☐
1985, 2 MAY PE34	**MAP OF THE PERSIAN GULF AREA IN 1965 (SS/31B)** Print 15,000 .... London EC; London IS CDS or m/c; other CDS .... from	1.00(S) 1.50(C)	0.35	☐	☐ ☐
1985, 7 MAY PE35	**RALPH VAUGHAN WILLIAMS (SS/32)** Based on the 1972 anniversaries 9p commemorative (European Music Year exhibition). Print 15,000 .... London EC 'National Stamp Day' spec. handstamp .... London EC or other CDS.....................................	1.00(S) 1.10(S) 1.25(C)	0.35	☐	☐ ☐ ☐
1985, 18 JUNE PE36	**LIFEBOAT RESCUE (SS/33)** Based on 2½d. International Lifeboat Conference commemorative of 1963 (Safety at Sea exhibition). Print 16,000 .... London, etc. special handstamps on 'Safety at Sea' commemoratives... London EC; Dover or other CDS; or 'FDI'	1.00(S) 1.10(S) 1.25(C)(F)	0.35	☐	☐ ☐ ☐
1985, 7 OCTOBER PE37	**'NIGHT MAIL' (SS/34)** Still from 1936 film of London-Scotland TPO; excerpt from commentary (PO Film Festival exhibition). Print 16,500 .... London EC; Down Special or other TPO CDS .... from	1.00(S) 1.25(C)	0.35	☐	☐ ☐
1985, 14 OCTOBER PE38	**£5 ORANGE OF 1882 (SS/35)** (RM Phillips Collection – new presentation). Print 17,000 .... London EC; London IS MLO or other CDS....... from.......	1.00(S) 1.25(C)	0.35	☐	☐ ☐

			FDI	Mint		

1986, 14 JANUARY

PE39 — **'DATAPOST' SALOON RACING CAR (SS/36)**
(British Motor Industry exhibition)
Print 17,200 .... 1.00(S) 0.35 ☐ ☐
London EC; Aberdeen or other CDS .... 1.25(C) ☐
London or other 'FDI' or special handstamps on Industry Year
commemoratives .... from 1.00(F)(S) ☐

1986, 4 MARCH

PE40 — **HALLEY'S COMET.** Not numbered.
Colour composite photo. of comet taken Dec. '85. Issued for Stampex '86.
Print 25,000 .... 1.00(S) 0.35 ☐ ☐
London EC; Edinburgh/19 or other CDS .... from 1.25(C) ☐

1986, 21 APRIL

PE41 — **DOROTHY WILDING PHOTOGRAPH OF THE QUEEN (SS/37)**
(60th Birthday of HM The Queen exhibition).
Print 20,000 .... 1.00(S) 0.35 ☐ ☐
London EC; London IS MLO or other CDS .... from 1.25(C) ☐
London or other 'FDI' or special handstamps on Queen's
Birthday commemoratives .... from 1.00(F)(S) ☐

1986, 6 MAY

PE42 — **1d. BLACK and 20c CERES BLACK (SS/38)**
GB 1d. Black of 1840 and France 20c Ceres Black of 1849.
Issued National Stamp Day (Joint exhibition by NPM and Paris Postal Museum).
Print 16,000 .... 1.00(S) 0.35 ☐ ☐
London EC; London IS MLO or other CDS .... from 1.25(C) ☐

1986, 20 MAY

PE43 — **SCAVENGING SEAGULLS (SS/39a)**
Photo. by Paul West, Saltburn (A winning entry of NPM/Creative Photography Magazine Nature Conservation Photographic competition).
Print 11,000 .... 1.00(S) 0.35 ☐ ☐
London EC or other CDS .... from 1.25(C) ☐
London or other 'FDI' or special handstamps on Nature Conservation commemoratives .... from 1.00(F)(S) ☐

1986, 20 MAY

PE44 — **DAMSELFLY (SS/39b)**
Photo. by Alex Cleland, Penicuik (A winning entry in photographic competition as SS/39a).
Print 11,000 .... 1.00(S) 0.35 ☐ ☐
London EC; Edinburgh/19 or other CDS .... from 1.25(C) ☐
London or other 'FDI' or special handstamps on Nature Conservation commemoratives .... from 1.00(F)(S) ☐

1986, 23 JUNE

PE45 — **INDIA POST 1843 – SS HINDOSTAN (SS/40)**
Painting of P&O vessel off Southampton (India-UK Mails exhibition).
Print 12,000 .... 1.00(S) 0.35 ☐ ☐
London EC or other CDS .... from 1.25(C) ☐
Southampton or other Philatelic Counter special handstamp 1.30(S) ☐

1986, 16 SEPTEMBER

PE46 — **BRISTOL FIGHTER AIRCRAFT (SS/41)**
From 1914-18 war. (Royal Air Force exhibition).
Print 11,000 .... 1.00(S) 0.35 ☐ ☐
London EC; Bristol or other 'FDI' or special handstamp on RAF
commemoratives .... from 1.10(F)(S) ☐
London EC; Bristol or other CDS .... from 1.25(C) ☐

1986, 14 OCTOBER

PE47 — **PORTRAIT OF QUEEN VICTORIA.** Not numbered.
By Heinrich von Angeli used for imprinted GPO postcards from 1889. (Postal Stationary exhibition).
Issued for British Philatelic Exhibition 1986.
Print number not yet released .... 1.00(S) 0.35 ☐ ☐
London SW1 '1986 British Phil. Exhib.' handstamp .... 1.00(S) ☐
London EC/31 or other CDS .... from 1.25(C) ☐

CENTENARY OF QUEEN VICTORIA'S GOLDEN JUBILEE
(Theme of main exhibition for 1987)

1987, 6 JANUARY

PE48 — **1887 'JUBILEE' 2d. (87/1)**
Colour trial and issued stamp.
Print number not yet released .... 1.00(S) 0.30 ☐ ☐

1987, 6 JANUARY

PE49 — **1887 'JUBILEE' 10d (87/2)**
Colour trial and issued stamp.
Print number not yet released .... 1.00(S) 0.30 ☐ ☐

			FDI	Mint	
1987, 6 JANUARY	**1887 'JUBILEE' 1/- (87/3)**				
	Colour trial and issued stamp.				
PE50	Print number not yet released...............................		1.00(S)	0.30	☐ ☐
PE48-50	Set of 3 as above		3.00(S)	0.90	☐ ☐

N.B. In 1987 two other sets of three cards are due to be issued in May and September.

Since 1980 the Museum has sold other cards not published by the Post Office — e.g. Cambridge Pillar Boxes; GWR TPO Coach No. 814, Didcot; 'Knee Deep' Fores painting; Early TPOs by R. Blake; Postage Label 16½p and 17p; etc.

PE22

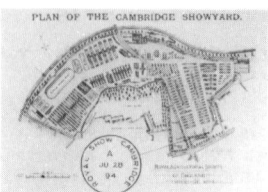
PE24

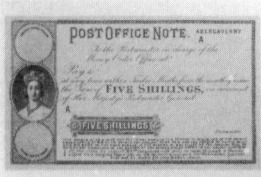
PE30

PE36

PE41

PE43

PE45

PE46

PE50

HQP16

HQP20

HQP22

Typesetting and origination by **MILBROOKE**, 13 Grace Hill, Folkestone, Kent Tel: Folkestone 0303 57255

Printed by **KPC PRINT** London and Ashford, Kent